Donald L. Griggs

Planning for Teaching Church School

- **·Identify Main Ideas**
- **·Determine Objectives**
- **·Design Teaching Activities**
- **·Select Resources**
- **·Organize Lesson Plan**

Judson Press ® Valley Forge

PLANNING FOR TEACHING CHURCH SCHOOL

Copyright © 1985
Judson Press, Valley Forge, PA 19482-0851

Second Printing, 1988

Library of Congress Cataloging in Publication Data

Griggs, Donald L.
  Planning for teaching church school.

   1. Christian education—Teaching methods—Handbooks,
manuals, etc.   I. Title.
BV1534.G737   1986   268'.4   85-12588
ISBN 0-8170-1079-3

The name JUDSON PRESS is registered as a trademark in the U.S. Patent Office.
Printed in the U.S.A.

Dedicated to the teachers, members, and staff of the First Presbyterian Church, Livermore, California, who first challenged me in 1964 to become a Christian educator and who continue to provide the context for meaningful ministry.

Contents

PART 1

A Planning Process

Introduction

This book approaches planning for teaching from five different perspectives. First of all, it responds to four specific questions that all church teachers ask of themselves and their curriculum when they approach the task of planning for teaching. Secondly, the book presents what I believe to be the essential components for devising an effective session plan for teaching a church school class. Third, this book can be viewed as an ''owner's manual,'' providing clear directions for the basic steps necessary for planning and teaching a typical session in the church school. Fourth, the book also summarizes a process that teachers can apply to the curriculum they use. This process is illustrated and implemented when the directions are followed for using one of the three sets of planning cards. Fifth, it is my intent that the reader approach this book as a dialogue between the reader and the author, as if we were working together as a team, planning for teaching next week's church school class.

Let's imagine that you and I are serving as a teaching team for one of the classes in our church. We have been teaching together for a little more than a year. We work well together and most of the time we enjoy being with members of our class. In our imaginary scenario you and I have come to the church because it is a convenient place to meet to plan for the next unit of four church school class sessions. As we sit together to plan our class sessions, we have our teacher's manuals, the student's book, our Bibles, and the other resources which are part of the curriculum our church has provided for us. We also have access to a variety of resources that are available to us in the church.

When we first started teaching, we wished that the curriculum was easier to use. We had presumed that because the curriculum was written and edited by experienced, professional church educators, all we would

have to do would be to follow the directions, do what they recommended, and all of our problems would be solved. We have since realized that those were unrealistic expectations. Church school curriculum at its best is only a tool, a resource for us to use to assist us with our planning. The problem with the curriculum is that the authors and editors never met us. They didn't know our situation, our students, our space, the amount of time we have, our particular interests and abilities, nor did they know our needs or the needs of our particular students. There is no way they could know all of this in order to write curriculum tailored to our situation. What they have had to do is write curriculum for a diverse, complex, mass market. What you and I have learned is that we must meet regularly in order to work with the curriculum in creative ways to adapt it to our situation.

As we work with our curriculum to plan for teaching, there are four questions that we have discovered help us to focus our planning. We respond to these questions in a very logical order.

1. What will we teach?
2. What will the learners accomplish?
3. What activities and resources will we plan?
4. What will be our overall strategy?

You will notice that Part One of the book devotes a chapter to each of these questions. These are the basic questions that all writers of curriculum and teachers of church school sessions ask of themselves in order to develop effective plans.

There is another way to look at planning for teaching, and that is to consider the essential components of a typical session plan. As we answer our four questions, we begin to identify those components as *main ideas* to communicate to the participants, *objectives* toward which we direct their learning, *activities* to involve the participants, *resources* to use to implement the activities, and a teaching *strategy* that incorporates five different parts of a lesson plan. When we can identify these components in our teachers' manuals and build our session plans on the basis of these components, we will find that the plan not only makes sense to us who teach it, but also to those who experience it as students. In the four chapters of Part One these essential components will be explored in clear, helpful ways.

This past summer I decided to install an automatic garage door opener in our house. The experience with that garage door opener is not unlike experiences I have had with church school curriculum. Perhaps my experience can be seen as a parable with which you may identify. My objective was to get a garage door opener that would be reliable, easy to install, provide additional security for our home, and enable us to leave and arrive with more ease.

I had seen a commercial on TV that claimed a person could install a garage door opener in an hour or two. Not being very handy with tools, I figured if it was that easy, surely I could do it. So I went shopping, found the one I wanted, brought it home, and opened the box. The first thing I found was the owner's manual. It contained diagrams, parts lists, troubleshooting advice, and eighteen steps to follow for proper installation. In large bold print at the top of page one I read, "READ ALL DIRECTIONS BEFORE PROCEEDING." Twenty-four pages later I had a general idea of what to do. I gathered the recommended tools and started with step one. As I completed the first few steps, I began to gain confidence. Then came the step of deciding where to place one of the brackets in order to have the proper leverage. I knew I needed help, so I called upon Jim, my good neighbor across the street, who had installed his own garage door opener some years earlier. With his help, with careful reading and following of all the directions, and with making an extension for one of the support brackets (Jim proved to be a helpful innovator in this area), Jim and I came to the fateful moment when we were to push the button to see if the opener worked. Lo and behold, miracle of miracles, the garage door went down and then up, automatically. After some minor adjustments and fine tuning, the garage door opener worked like a charm.

The whole project was a success due to several factors: I had the necessary tools and knew how to use them; the directions were clearly written with helpful diagrams; I took the time necessary to read all the directions and did each step without making assumptions or taking short-cuts; I had the assistance and encouragement of a good neighbor; and we were willing to adapt the directions for my situation. Even though the project was not as easy as the TV commercial led me to believe, I discovered that there was great personal satisfaction in accomplishing the task successfully.

There are several factors that influence the successful planning of lessons for church school. The curriculum is in many ways like an "owner's manual." There are several specific steps that must be taken in planning for teaching. The four chapters of Part One represent four steps that I believe are crucial to the planning process. Whether or not our teacher's manual itself specifies these steps in the same way, it is possible for us to apply the four steps to our own curriculum as we plan for teaching.

I am sure that if I had observed someone install a garage door opener before I installed mine, it would have been a little easier for me the first time. I am also sure that if I were to install another one, it would be easier the next time. With practice comes familiarity and with familiarity comes confidence. The same is true in planning for teaching: the more we practice the steps in the planning process, the more confident we will become and the more quickly we will be able to accomplish the task. In order to provide an opportunity to practice the steps in the process of planning for teaching, Part Two includes directions for using three sets of planning cards. Following the directions step by step and using one set of cards at a time, it is possible for us, individually or in teams of two or three, to practice the process of planning for teaching. After practicing the process, we can then apply the same steps and the same skills to the curriculum our church has provided. If we are patient with ourselves, with each other, and with the curriculum, we will find that our confidence will increase week by week. If we realize that the published curriculum is at best a helpful resource and that we must take the time and the effort to adapt it to our own situation, then we will find ourselves less frustrated when what is written in the teacher's manual is not directly appropriate to our class. And, if we will follow several essential steps in the planning process, we may find that not only do we receive more satisfaction from our teaching but also those whom we teach are more involved, more enthusiastic, and more successful in their own learning.

I wish that it would be possible actually to sit down with you to plan for the series of sessions you will be teaching the next few weeks. Obviously that is an impossibility. However, it is possible with this book to share with you the insights, the procedures, and the skills that I have discovered and developed as a teacher in the church in the past thirty years. If you are working alone with this book, thank you for inviting me to join you in the process of planning. If you are a group of teachers working together, thank you for including me as a part of your team as we work together through the steps of planning for teaching.

CHAPTER 1

What Will We Teach?

As we think about teaching our class, the first question we want to consider is, "What are we going to teach?" We have about forty-five minutes each week to interact with the members of our class. At first impression forty-five minutes doesn't seem to be very much time to accomplish anything of significance. However, those forty-five minutes could be very worthwhile if they were carefully planned and effectively implemented. The important first step is to focus clearly on what we intend to communicate to our students.

When we try to identify what we are going to teach, we often refer to it as the content or subject matter of the session, or we may refer to a specific Bible story or passage. Another way to summarize what we are to teach is to speak of it as the focus of the lesson. In the various church curricula the focus of the lesson will be described by one of many different words: topic, theme, lesson summary, Bible emphasis, or key concept. Each curriculum will have its own way of identifying and summarizing what is to be the focus of the session. For the purposes of this book and in order to be consistent, I will use the term "main idea" to represent the few words that will capture the essence of our answer to the question "What will we teach?"

A main idea is a brief statement that expresses clearly what the focus of a particular session will be. Obviously in a class session we share much more than a brief statement. We read verses, paragraphs, and pages. We discuss together what we think and believe. We develop the main idea in a variety of ways. However, when we express in our own words, in a few sentences, the essence of what we want to communicate to the students, we are able to do a better job of planning the whole lesson.

There are several sources from which we receive clues as to the main idea that we will teach in a given session.

The session plan in the teacher's manual has a summary of the topic. This summary can be as brief as one paragraph or as long as a page. Whether brief or long, the summary usually expresses quite clearly what the author/editor intended for us to focus on for that session. The Bible passage on which the session is based will provide ample evidence of what we should emphasize in our teaching. Stories and illustrations, whether biblical, fiction, or nonfiction, that are included as resources in the session plans will also provide sufficient clues as to what the focus of our teaching should be. One other very important source from which we derive the main idea of a session is our own personal experiences of faith and life that are related to the session topic, the Bible passage, or other suggested material in the session plan. From these four sources and others we teachers will be able to determine our own responses to the question "What will we teach?"

This first step in the planning process—stating clearly what we understand to be the main idea of the session—is a very necessary step on which the rest of the planning process depends heavily. There are several criteria to keep in mind as we identify the main idea for each session we teach.

Write the Main Idea in Your Own Words

When we come face to face with the students in our class, it is very important that we share with them something that is personally meaningful to us. It is not enough just to read what the author/editor writes and then try to share that with the students. We need to think through what the author/editor has written, relate that to other things we know, and make connections with our own faith and life experiences. Students will be more influenced to learn and grow when they encounter teachers who have genuine convictions about what they think, feel, and believe. As we begin our planning for teaching by answering the question "What will we teach?" it is essential that we express the main idea of the session by writing it out in our own words. With such a prepared statement it will be easier to take the next steps in the planning process.

Be Selective—Focus on What Is Possible

There is so much to teach and we have so little time. The teacher's manual often suggests more than seems possible for one brief session. As we work at expressing the main idea of the session, it is more helpful to the students and to ourselves to focus on what we want to communicate rather than trying to present everything related to a subject. Instead of trying to cover everything that is suggested, we will be more effective if we work at uncovering something specific, worthwhile, and relevant for us and our students at this particular time. We should try to accomplish what is manageable in a given session and not feel guilty about those good things we could not cover. It is better for the students to feel that they have accomplished something specific than to feel frustrated because information was presented to them too quickly and superficially.

Be Sure the Main Idea Is Appropriate to the Learner

As adult teachers we have had a lot of time and many opportunities to think about the subjects we are teaching to those in our class. We have usually come to some conclusions and convictions about significant matters related to faith and life. We are often tempted to share our conclusions and convictions with the students without allowing them time to work through these faith and life problems for themselves. Important words such as "faith," "salvation," "justice," "grace," "peace," and many others are abstract words. Adults can identify tangible experiences to express what these words mean to us. Children, youth, and some adults may not be able to comprehend what such words mean—they may not have tangible experiences to connect with such abstract concepts. As we prepare the main idea for a session, it is important to keep in mind the intellectual, emotional, and spiritual development and readiness of our students. We need to see the main idea for the session through the eyes of those whom we teach.

Relate the Main Idea to the Bible

The Bible is the primary source book for our teaching

in the church. Almost all church school curriculum is designed to communicate the message of the Bible. Even when the curriculum emphasizes church history, denominational matters, or social issues, there is usually an effort made to undergird those subjects with biblical references. In writing the main idea, remember how important it is to express as succinctly as possible the essence of the biblical text that is emphasized for a particular lesson.

Relate the Main Idea to Life Experiences

We do not study and teach the Bible for its own sake alone. Rather, we study and teach the Bible so that it will have some impact on our lives—the way we think, feel, believe, and act. If what we are teaching from the Bible doesn't have any relationship to our faith and life, then we should question whether there is sufficient justification to teach it. The main idea should be written in such a way that there is some indication of what aspect of life experience will be focused on in the session.

Write the Main Idea Clearly and Succinctly

Even though we are writing the main idea for our own personal benefit, to help us as we plan for a particular lesson, it is important to write as clearly and succinctly as possible. If the main idea is written in a complex, confusing style, it is quite possible that the subject will appear to be equally complex and confusing to the students. The clearer the main idea the more likely we will understand what we are trying to communicate.

Express the Main Idea as an Affirmation of What We Believe

The main idea should represent something that we teachers have some convictions about and feel motivated to teach. When what we teach is something we believe in, we can teach with enthusiasm and the students become aware that what we teach them is something we believe in for ourselves. This does not mean that we teach in such an autocratic, authoritarian style that we overwhelm the students with our beliefs. Rather, it means that we express what we think, feel, and believe in such a way that the students know where we stand and at the same time feel free to express themselves in their own personal ways.

Sample Main Ideas

The following examples of main ideas were written by teachers using a published church school curriculum. In each instance the teacher's manual did not have a clearly, succinctly written main idea. However, the curriculum contained helpful clues regarding the main idea of the session. Following the guidelines outlined above, the teachers worked on writing main ideas for their lessons that would be appropriate for their students and serve as a basis for developing the rest of the session plan.

Main idea for the class of three-year-olds:

The church is a place where young children are welcomed and nurtured. Children feel like they belong to the church when they can share experiences and relationships with their church friends. Being friends means sharing, doing things together, taking turns, and helping one another.

Main idea for second- and third-grade class:

In the beginning God created human beings to share all of God's creation with one another and with God. God created men and women and boys and girls with the abilities to create ideas and objects, to understand ideas and how things work, and to work together with God as partners in creation. Everything that is created has a name and a purpose.

Main idea for fifth- and sixth-grade class:

Persons experience conflicts and struggles as well as reconciliation and joys in their relationships with one another and with God. Jacob, Isaac's son and Esau's brother, experienced conflict, struggle, reconciliation, and joy which are focused in two encounters with God in the desert and one encounter with Esau. The encounters with God and Esau are presented in three stories which feature a ladder, a wrestling match, and a warm embrace.

Main idea for junior high school class:

There are different kinds of power and authority present in the church today, as there were also in the early church. There is power and authority through the Holy Spirit; in the words of Scripture; in spoken words; in groups as they meet, discuss, and make decisions; and in persons who are leaders as well as followers. With power comes responsibility for serving God and serving persons. Young people in the church have some power and responsibility for helping the church to be a faithful witness to God's good news.

Now that you have some guidelines for writing main ideas and have seen some examples of main ideas written by other teachers, you are ready to try your hand at writing main ideas for your own situation. Spend time with your teacher's manual by yourself or with a co-teacher. Look for all the clues that suggest the main idea of the session. Work at writing a main idea for next week's lesson. After you have written a main idea, return to the guidelines presented earlier in order to evaluate what you have written. For the purpose of developing your skill, try rewriting the main idea so that you will have something that you feel represents the best you can do. You will find that after practice you will be able to write main ideas quite quickly.

CHAPTER 2

What Will the Learners Accomplish?

After we have summarized with the main idea what we desire to communicate to the students, there is a second question to which we must respond: ''What will the learners accomplish?'' By stating the main idea, we have expressed what we as teachers desire to communicate to the learners. In taking the second step in the planning process, we are attempting to identify those things that we intend for the learners to accomplish as a result of participating in the lesson we present. We must keep a definite intention in mind.

All teachers' manuals that I have seen answer the question in one way or another. Sometimes the intentions of a lesson are identified as *aims*. Other times they may be expressed as *desired outcomes*. I have also seen curriculum in which the intentions are stated as *purposes*. Whatever they are called, they show that the author/ editor of the curriculum has something in mind that the students should accomplish in a particular church school session. Again, in order to be consistent and clear I choose to describe these aims, purposes, or outcomes as *objectives*. We will plan for the learners to accomplish one or more objectives based upon the main idea that we have developed.

An *objective* is a clear statement that describes in specific, observable terms what we teachers desire for the students to be able to accomplish by the end of the session that they could not do at the beginning. There are at least three reasons for writing objectives for each teaching session: (1) they provide a focus and direction for our planning, (2) they assure us that the selections of specific teaching activities and resources will be more purposeful, and (3) they provide a basis for us to evaluate if we and the students have achieved our intent. Objectives help us prepare the session as well as evaluate it.

Objectives are to be distinguished from goals.

Goals	Objectives
Tend to be general	Tend to be specific
Are large, i.e., encompassing	Are small, i.e., limited
Provide a basis for evaluating a whole curriculum or educational program	Provide a basis for evaluating particular units or sessions
Are worth spending a lifetime pursuing	Are achievable in a given instructional setting
Incorporate the whole of the learning process	Are applicable to individual students in particular activities
Give direction for the broad scope of the educational enterprise	Give direction for planning given units and sessions
Are long-range	Are short-range
Are partially achievable	Are completely achievable

Goals are important for the overall program of Christian education, for evaluating and selecting curriculum, and for providing a frame of reference to judge whether or not particular objectives are worthwhile. As important as goals are, they are not very helpful when trying to plan a particular lesson for one forty-five-minute session. Perhaps an illustration of a goal and an objective related to the same subject will illustrate more clearly the difference between the two.

A goal of Christian education is to nurture persons so that they may know, love, use, and live with the Bible as the word of God.

An objective for a church school session with fifth- and sixth-graders is that they will: bring their own Bibles to class, find a passage that describes what Jesus expects of his disciples, and express in their own words what it means to be disciples of Jesus today.

The issue is not whether objectives are better than goals. Rather, the issue is when are goals more helpful and when are objectives more helpful? Our concern in this book, and especially this chapter, is to develop effective ways to plan for specific church school sessions. In that context, objectives will be more helpful to us in our planning.

Much has been written and spoken about the advantages and disadvantages of working with objectives. In both public education and religious education circles, there has often been too much of an emphasis on the technical aspects of writing and being accountable for objectives. It is quite possible to become convinced that objectives are necessary for planning a lesson and then to place unnecessary restrictions and limitations on the teaching and the learning. I would resist all attempts to get too technical about writing and utilizing objectives. I recognize that there are some liabilities to objectives when too much emphasis is placed on them or when too much is expected. Some of the liabilities are:

Outcomes that are easily described are often unimportant.

Stating objectives prior to teaching may discourage teachers from being spontaneous and flexible.

Objectives may emphasize information, facts, dates, and other details and neglect important matters such as ideas, values, feelings, and beliefs.

The achievement of objectives may deceive the teacher into thinking that learning what it means to be Christian has been accomplished.

It takes time to prepare objectives for each session.

Recognizing that there are potential pitfalls, I am still an advocate for writing objectives for each church school session. I do not want to get too technical with objectives, nor do I want to insist that a prescribed number of criteria be met when writing objectives. I do not want to presume that when objectives have been achieved by the students, we have accomplished everything that is important in terms of learning and growing in the Christian faith. I am an advocate for using objectives as part of the process of planning for teaching because:

By writing objectives, teachers are helped in thinking through the necessary steps that must be taken to accomplish larger goals.

When objectives arise out of the main idea, there develops a very clear focus for the session.

With objectives clearly stated it is possible to make more appropriate selections of teaching activities and resources that will be most effective.

Objectives can be shared with some students so that they have a clearer perspective on what is expected of them.

Guided by objectives, we realize it is possible that the plan for the whole session will be more coherent and develop in a more effective way.

In chapter 1 were examples of main ideas that show how four different teachers expressed what they desired to communicate with their respective classes. Those same teachers prepared objectives related to the main ideas.

Objectives for class of three-year-olds:
During the session the children will:
1. Participate happily and cooperatively in an activity center.
2. Relate to a story about sharing and taking turns.
3. Name at least two other children who are their church friends.
4. Express in their own ways what it means to be a friend.

Objectives for second- and third-grade class:
During the session the children will:
1. Express in their own ways their understanding of God as Creator.
2. Identify by their names a variety of things that God created.
3. Participate in one or more activities that involve them as creators.
4. Retell in their own words a portion of the creation story from Genesis 2:4-23.
5. Explain what it means to be partners with God and one another in creation.

Objectives for fifth- and sixth-grade class:
During the session the children will:
1. Name the persons on the family tree from Abraham and Sarah to Jacob's children.
2. Trace on a map the journey of Jacob.
3. Retell in their own words at least one of the two stories of Jacob's encounters with God at Bethel or the Jabbok River.
4. Describe the encounter between Jacob and Esau

and explain what the word "reconciliation" means.

5. Express in a creative way their interpretations of Jacob's encounters with God and Esau.
6. Identify times in their own lives when they have experienced conflicts, struggles, joys, and reconciliation with God and/or other persons close to them.

Objectives for seventh- to ninth-grade class:
During the session the youth will be able to:

1. Describe the nature of power that was present in the early church as evidenced by Acts 5.
2. Explore ways power is present and exercised in their own church.
3. Identify places and ways in which they may be able to relate to the structures or sources of power in their church.
4. Decide on something to do as a group, or as individuals, to participate in the ministry of their church.
5. Explain the relationships between power and responsibility.

As you read these examples of objectives you will notice that each one begins with a word that is very specific. These verbs are descriptive of actions that students can do in order to demonstrate what they have accomplished in the course of the class session. Not all students will accomplish all objectives with equal success. Not all objectives will be accomplished in every class session. However, the objectives do serve as bench marks, or as targets, to help the teachers in their planning.

Something else you will notice about the preceding four sets of objectives is that in each set there are two or more types or levels of objectives. The third set is a good example of this point. There is quite a difference between "naming" persons on a family tree, "retelling" in their own words, and "identifying" items in their own lives. When you write objectives for a session or unit, it is important to include as many types of objectives as possible.

I have attempted to identify six different types of objectives. These categories may be somewhat arbitrary, but I believe that there is a clear rationale for including these six in the order that they are presented, a rationale which is explained as I delineate each type of objective.

REMEMBERING. This is the first step toward learning. Before one can do anything else with information, there must be some degree of remembering. We make a mistake if we presume that remembering equals learning.

Actually, remembering equals remembering. This is a very important step, but it is only the first step. Words we could use for writing objectives to emphasize remembering are: Define . . . Describe . . . Find . . . List . . . Locate . . . Match . . . Name . . . Recall . . . Retell.

COMPARING. After we have remembered important information about several subjects, we can then do comparisons to see the similarities and differences between the subjects. Comparing activities requires the skill of analysis, which is a step greater than remembering. Words to use for writing objectives to emphasize comparing are: Analyze . . . Categorize . . . Contrast . . . Debate . . . Differentiate . . . Distinguish . . . Outline . . . Relate . . . Review.

INTERPRETING. When students are asked, "What is the meaning of . . . ?" they are invited to engage in a process of interpretation. It is not enough to accumulate a lot of information. It is a very important step in the learning process to seek meaning beyond the information. Every church school session should incorporate one or more activities that encourage students to work at interpretation. Words we could use for writing objectives to emphasize interpreting are: Conclude . . . Discuss . . . Explain . . . Illustrate . . . Interpret . . . Question . . . Synthesize . . . Translate . . . Summarize.

CREATING. Students show evidence of having learned about a subject when they are able to express by some creative means what their understanding is of that subject. By being encouraged to express themselves creatively, the students are able to think through a subject, internalize it for themselves, and bring forth something that is personally important and satisfying. In their creativity they are able to express their ideas, values, feelings, and beliefs. There are many forms of creative expression. Words we could use for writing objectives to emphasize creating are: Construct . . . Create . . . Design . . . Dramatize . . . Draw . . . Express . . . Illustrate . . . Revise . . . Speak . . . Write.

RELATING to one's experiences. A significant next step in the learning process is when persons are able to make connections between what they are studying and their own experiences, as well as the experiences of others in their world. It is not sufficient to remember Bible passages about forgiveness, or to compare Old and New Testament concepts of forgiveness, or to interpret and express one's understanding of forgiveness in creative ways. It is important to enable students to relate what they are studying to their own experiences of forgiveness. Words we could use for writing objectives to emphasize relating to one's experiences are: Apply . . . Connect . . . Identify with . . . Observe . . . Relate . . . See . . . Show.

INFLUENCING one's values, beliefs, and actions. The goal of learning is to influence persons' values, beliefs, and actions, not just to instruct, indoctrinate, or reinforce particular categories of information. Teachers in the church are seeking to be agents of God who help others to learn about their relationship to God and especially to live as Christians in the world. If our teaching does not invite others to put into practice what they are learning, then we are neglecting something very important. Words we could use for writing objectives to emphasize influencing one's values, beliefs, and actions are: Choose . . . Decide . . . Help . . . Join . . . Participate . . . Serve . . . Use . . . Volunteer . . . Work.

In the course of a unit's study it is necessary to plan for a wide variety of activities so that all six types of objectives, representing six aspects of the learning process, are included. It is easier to plan activities that emphasize remembering, comparing, and interpreting. Most curriculum resources feature activities of these types. It is more difficult to devise lessons that feature creating, relating, and influencing activities; yet it is with these types of activities that the most significant learning occurs.

CHAPTER 3

What Activities and Resources Will We Plan?

We have already accomplished two important steps in our planning for teaching a church school session. We have stated the *main idea* of the session and we have identified *objectives* related to the main idea. Now that we have determined what we want to communicate to the learners and have identified what we expect them to accomplish, it is necessary to take the next step. The means for communicating the main ideas and accomplishing the objectives are the *teaching activities* and *resources* we will utilize.

Teaching Activities are those procedures which teachers devise to guide student involvement with the subject of the session. Activities are often referred to as methods.

Resources, also called materials, are those objects that teachers and students use in order to implement the activities. Resources are mechanical in the form of recorders and projectors, conceptual in the form of pho-

1. Verbal symbols: words

2. Visual symbols: maps, charts, photographs

3. Audio symbols: records, cassettes, radio

4. Audiovisual symbols: films, filmstrips, videotapes

5. Exhibits: displays, artifacts

6. Field trips: church building, neighborhood, other churches

7. Demonstrations: by experts in local church or community

8. Dramatizations: plays, puppets, pantomimes

9. Contrived experiences: role playing, simulations

10. Direct, purposeful, personal experiences

*Edgar Dale, *Audiovisual Methods in Teaching,* 3rd ed. (New York: Holt, Rinehart and Winston, Inc., 1946, 1954, 1969). Reprinted by permission of CBS College Publishing.

tographs and maps, and verbal in the form of a series of questions. The most valuable resources are the persons present.

There are many ways to categorize the various types of activities and resources. Edgar Dale, of Ohio State University, constructed what has become known as Dale's Cone of Learning.* This cone is composed of ten sections with the small section (1) at the peak and the largest section (10) at the base. Each of the ten sections of the cone represents a different type of teaching activity and resource. The movement from top to bottom is a movement from the more abstract to the more concrete, from less involvement by the students to more direct involvement. (The movement from abstract to concrete is similar to the development of the six types of objectives, beginning with remembering and ending with influencing one's values, beliefs, and actions.) The ten categories of Dale's Cone of Learning are:

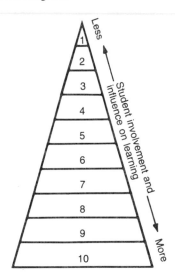

If we take seriously Dale's Cone of Learning, then we need to consider a wide variety of activities over a period of time in order to involve all the students with their diverse needs, interests, and abilities. As we plan our lessons week by week, we need to consider how we can incorporate activities and resources in the lessons that represent all the sections of the cone, especially the lower half of the cone.

There is another way to look at various types of teaching activities and resources. Instead of viewing the categories vertically, moving down the cone from least to most effective, we can view the categories horizontally along a continuum. At one end of the continuum are the most structured, didactic activities and at the other end are the most open-ended, serendipitous activities.

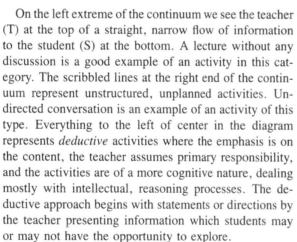

On the left extreme of the continuum we see the teacher (T) at the top of a straight, narrow flow of information to the student (S) at the bottom. A lecture without any discussion is a good example of an activity in this category. The scribbled lines at the right end of the continuum represent unstructured, unplanned activities. Undirected conversation is an example of an activity of this type. Everything to the left of center in the diagram represents *deductive* activities where the emphasis is on the content, the teacher assumes primary responsibility, and the activities are of a more cognitive nature, dealing mostly with intellectual, reasoning processes. The deductive approach begins with statements or directions by the teacher presenting information which students may or may not have the opportunity to explore.

All that is to the right of the center represents *inductive* activities where there is considerable concern for the process in which the students are involved, where students assume more responsibility for their learning, and the activities are more affective in nature, dealing with feelings, values, and beliefs. The inductive approach begins with a note of inquiry where questions, problems,

and issues are provided so that students may be motivated to explore the subject in order to arrive at their own conclusions.

One of the reasons for viewing teaching activities and resources on a continuum of various degrees of deductive and inductive emphases is to suggest that effective teaching will incorporate all the elements of the continuum. It is not a matter of one side of the continuum being positive and the other side negative. Rather, it is the case that there are times when a deductive approach will be the most useful and at other times the inductive approach is preferred. The most effective teaching will include a blend and balance between both approaches. One session may include more deductive activities and another session more of the inductive type, but over a unit of sessions there should be a good balance.

As I have considered activities and resources, I have devised another set of ten categories. Some of the categories are similar to those of Dale's Cone of Learning. Other categories are related to the six types of objectives I outlined in chapter 2. All the categories represent various aspects of the deductive-inductive continuum. Each of the ten categories is described briefly and then illustrated with two or more examples. All the examples are based on passages from the Gospel of Mark. They are written succinctly, providing enough information to suggest how the activity might be presented. In order to use the activities in an actual class setting, it would be necessary to develop them further with more details and clearer directions. The activities as outlined here could be most appropriately adapted for older children through adults. The ten categories of teaching activities and resources are:

1. Verbalizing
2. Comparing and Analyzing
3. Reading and Exploring
4. Choosing, Searching, and Responding
5. Responding to Filmstrips
6. Using Audio Cassettes
7. Dramatizing
8. Creating Personal Expressions
9. Relating to Personal Experiences
10. Direct Personal Experiences

Verbalizing Activities and Resources

Brainstorming is an open-ended process which involves a quick listing of ideas, questions, or suggestions without comment or evaluation. Brainstorming involves the whole group.

Following are examples of three topics that could be

used as a basis for brainstorming:

1. Let's make a list of all the persons we can think of who were friends and followers of Jesus.
2. When you think of disciples and apostles, what are some characteristics or qualities of these persons that come to mind?
3. On the day after Jesus' crucifixion what are some concerns or questions the followers of Jesus might have had?

Write down as many suggestions and responses as are offered in five to ten minutes. After you make a list, it is important to work with each item to decide whether or not to keep it on the list, understand its importance in relation to other suggestions, or explore it further.

Questions that encourage analytical thinking are an excellent verbal activity and resource. Such questions are more open-ended and allow for many possible appropriate answers.

Some examples of analytical questions include:

1. Why do you suppose Jesus' first response to the paralytic was, ''My son, your sins are forgiven''?
2. When Jesus answered the teacher of the Law by saying, ''You are not far from the kingdom of God'' (Mark 12:34), what do you think he meant?
3. What are some possible interpretations of the parable of the tenants in the vineyard?

Interviews are another excellent verbal activity. Teachers can interview special guests. Students can prepare a list of questions to use in an interview of the minister or other church leaders. Students can conduct ''man on the street'' interviews of persons as they arrive for church (prior notification of church members of this activity would be helpful). Students can do individual or small group research projects, then interview each other.

Comparing and Analyzing

Questions can be used to guide the process of comparing and analyzing. Some examples are:

1. When you compare the resurrection narrative in Mark with the same narrative of the other three Gospels, what are some similarities and differences you notice?
2. What relationship do you see between Psalm 22 and the passion of Jesus at the crucifixion?

Directions can be given to encourage students to compare and analyze various passages of Scripture. An example:

Find at least six passages where Jesus is functioning as a teacher.

1. Whom was Jesus teaching?

2. What was Jesus' message?
3. What was the response of the people to Jesus?
4. What do we learn about Jesus and the people?

A *story* about the apostle Peter can be presented by the teacher telling it, with a filmstrip, or by the students reading the story. After encountering the story, students can compare Peter with another apostle, compare an event early in Peter's association with Jesus with his denial of Jesus, or analyze the personality traits of Peter reflected in Mark's Gospel.

Reading and Exploring

Skimming is a reading skill that youth and adults are capable of performing. Students can be directed to skim one chapter of the Gospel of Mark (each student working with a different chapter) looking for something specific.

1. Look for the miracles of Jesus. With each miracle you find, answer several questions: Who is involved? What is the problem or need? How does Jesus respond to the need? What is the result?
2. Look for all the references to the disciples with Jesus. Who is present? What is their relationship to Jesus or to others? How does Jesus relate to the disciples?

Reading a specific passage, the students can be guided to accomplish several tasks:

1. Read and underline key words to look up in a Bible dictionary.
2. Write brief definitions in your own words.
3. With these definitions in mind explain what the passage means to you.

Using Bible study resources, such as dictionaries, concordances, atlases, or commentaries, the students can work with a passage in order to gather information, find parallel passages, determine the significance of the geographical setting, and develop their own interpretation.

Choosing, Searching, and Responding

Following are two examples of ways to engage students in making choices, searching for information, and responding creatively.

1. Some key persons in the Gospel of Mark are:

Levi (Matthew)	Peter	John the Baptist	Jairus
	Andrew	Woman who anointed	
		Jesus' feet	

Directions: Choose one person to study and think about, then:

—Use available resources to find some passages

and information about your person.
—Consider three questions:

What were some experiences of ___?
What problems or conflicts did ___encounter?
How did ___relate to Jesus?

—Write a brief letter of recommendation for your person, requesting that he or she be chosen as a spokesperson for Jesus. Or write a letter as if you are the person, to introduce yourself to someone who has asked questions about Jesus.

2. There are several important encounters between Jesus and other persons in the Gospel of Mark:

Mark 1:21-28	A man with an evil spirit
Mark 3:31-35	Jesus' mother and brothers
Mark 6:1-56	Jesus in Nazareth
Mark 10:17-31	The rich man
Mark 14:53-65	Jesus before the Council

Directions: Choose one of the encounters to study, then:
— Read the passage and refer to helpful resources.
— Consider several questions as you read:
Who were the persons involved?
What was the reason for the encounter?
What problems or conflicts were experienced?
What were the responses of Jesus? of the persons?
— Meet with others who studied the same encounter.
— Prepare a way to share your passage with the whole group. Choose one of the following:
News report from several reporters
A role play of the meeting
A journal of the ''minutes'' of the meeting

Responding to Filmstrips

Filmstrips are an effective means for *introducing new subjects*. There are several approaches that can be used:

1. Instruct students to look for something specific. When they have a reason to view the filmstrip, they will be more observant.
2. Before viewing a filmstrip, the class members could brainstorm all they know about the subject.
3. Part of the group could focus on one or two questions. The rest of the group could focus on something else. After viewing the filmstrip, they will be ready for a good discussion.

Filmstrips can be used in *various settings*. It is not necessary for a whole class to view a filmstrip together. Some optional settings include:

1. learning centers for presenting information
2. small groups who are exploring a subject
3. individuals who choose to pursue a particular topic
4. a presentation activity for early arrivals
5. an extra activity for those who finish early

Students can *create their own scripts* for filmstrips. After they have explored a subject enough to be familiar with it, students can use a filmstrip, without the script, to create their own caption or narration for each frame. Small groups or individuals can work at this task.

Instead of showing filmstrips from frame one to the end, it is possible to stop at an appropriate place in order to lead students in a *discussion of possible endings*.

Using Audio Cassettes

Listening to a portion of the Gospel of Mark is a way to present Scripture to poor readers. (The American Bible Society has complete recorded sets of cassettes of the New Testament in several translations.)

Teachers can *record directions* for activities in a learning center or for a small group. That way several groups can work on different tasks simultaneously without the teacher having to be present seemingly in several places at once.

Students can *record reports* to share with the group, scripts they have written for filmstrips or dramatizations, and stories they have created.

Tape recorders can be used to conduct ''live'' or simulated *interviews* based upon themes, events, or persons from the Gospel of Mark.

Songs and hymns sung by the choir, sung by a soloist, or played by the organist can be prerecorded to use as an accompaniment for singing in the classroom.

Dramatizing Activities and Resources

Puppets can be used by the teacher to present a story, to engage students in conversation, or to illustrate and interpret a biblical or theological concept. Students can use the puppets to interact with others, to tell a story they have read and discussed, or to express their own ideas and feelings.

Informal dramatizations are a good way to involve students in reviewing and retelling biblical narratives as well as other stories. Many biblical narratives can easily be developed into an informal dramatization.

Role play is a way for students to express their own ideas and feelings in response to a hypothetical situation either from the past or present.

Personal identification is what happens when students are guided to enter into a biblical story or event and speak in the first person from the perspective of a key character in the story. They see and think as that person.

Creating Personal Expressions

When students are invited to express their ideas, feelings, and beliefs, they engage in a very creative process. Much learning is reinforced and internalized when opportunities for creative expression are provided. There are many, many media, forms, and processes for creating personal expressions.

A selection of *photo slides* can be used to illustrate the meaning of a biblical passage in contemporary images.

With *blank transparent slides* which can be written and drawn on, students can create a set of visual images to express their understanding of one of the stories from the Gospel of Mark.

Magazine photographs are an excellent resource for creating montages, posters, and bulletin board displays. They can also be mounted and laminated to have as a permanent collection.

By using *overhead transparencies* students and teachers can draw and project illustrations, symbols, maps, litanies, songs, charts, and other visual images.

Creative writing activities include many possibilities:

— A page in the diary at the end of an imaginary day.
— A telegram to be sent to imaginary persons
— A memo from one follower of Jesus to another
— A job description of a follower of Jesus
— A news flash from the wires of Radio Jerusalem
— A letter requesting information or asking questions
— A poem to focus the essence of the meaning of a topic
— An editorial in the Jerusalem Journal
— An article by an investigative reporter

Relating to Personal Experiences

Questions can be asked that encourage students to relate the subject they are studying to their own lives. Some examples are:

When is a time you felt ''on the spot'' like Peter did when he was asked by Jesus, ''Who do you say that I am?''

If you had been in Levi's place, what would you have done when Jesus asked you to follow him?

What are some ways we experience being called to be Jesus' followers today?

When someone identifies you as a follower of Jesus, what are some feelings and responses you experience?

In the opening of the class session the students can be invited to reflect on personal experiences that have some connection with the topic of that session.

Before presenting the story of Jesus' call of the disciples, the teacher can ask the students to think about leaders that they follow in school, in the neighborhood, in the church, or in their family. Time can be spent discussing: Why do people need leaders? What are the responsibilities of followers? What would you want to know ahead of time before you decide to follow a leader?

Before discussing any of the miracles of Jesus, the students can be asked to think about experiences they have had or that their families or friends have had of which they could say, ''It was like a miracle.''

Before reflecting on Peter's denial of Jesus, the students can identify times in their own lives when they made promises that later they didn't keep.

By such reflection and discussion the students are better prepared to explore the biblical passage and to see ways that the passage relates to their own experiences.

Through *role play, creative writing, discussion,* and *simulations* the students can relate some of their own experiences to the subject they are studying. The experiences of biblical, historical, as well as contemporary persons are not unlike the experiences the students have in terms of their feelings, values, dynamics of relationships, and beliefs. When students can see the connections between their own lives and the lives of persons they are studying, they will be helped in their growing and learning.

Direct Personal Experiences

It is very difficult to plan direct personal experiences for each church school session. Not all biblical or theological subjects lend themselves to direct experience. However, there are ways that students can become involved in experiencing directly some of the topics they are studying.

If the topic of the session is forgiveness based on Jesus' parable of the unforgiving servant, it is possible to encourage the students to try to be intentionally forgiving of someone else during the week: a brother or sister, a parent, a friend, someone who is not a friend, or a stranger.

If the topic of the session is prayer and praying, the students can become involved in writing and speaking prayers during the class session and writing short prayers and spending a brief time each day in prayer at home.

If the topic of the session is disciples and discipleship, the students can be guided to think about what is expected of disciples of Jesus in terms of the way they live. They can decide on one or two specific things they will do during the week to live as disciples of Jesus.

If the biblical passage of the session is the Great Commandment, it is possible to discuss and then decide specific ways to express love for God, love for neighbor, and love for oneself.

Even though it may not always be possible to devise a learning activity that provides direct personal experience of the subject of the session, it is important in our planning always to raise the question "Is there any way during the session, or during the next week, that we can have a direct personal experience of what we are studying in this lesson?"

Criteria for Evaluating Teaching Activities and Resources

Given the multitude of possible teaching activities and resources, how does a teacher decide which ones to utilize in a given class session? How does a teacher know afterwards whether or not the activities and resources have accomplished what was intended? There are at least ten criteria that can be used to evaluate activities and resources. The activities and resources should:

1. help the teacher communicate clearly the main idea that was stated at the beginning of the planning process.
2. help the students accomplish the objectives that were intended for the session.
3. be presented with clear, helpful directions and followed up with encouragement by the teachers.
4. involve students in active and purposeful ways.
5. be those in which the teacher has some confidence.
6. allow for maximum creative expression on the part of the students.
7. represent a variety of skills and interests so that students can make choices from alternatives.
8. lead students to ask questions, seek answers, and state conclusions.
9. be appropriate to the time available and the space in which the class meets.
10. be appropriate to the developmental stage of the students as well as to the number who are present.

CHAPTER 4

What Will Be Our Overall Strategy?

In the previous three chapters we have answered three important questions and taken three necessary steps on our way to planning the lessons for our church school classes. By determining the main ideas, objectives, activities, and resources, we have all the raw material needed to complete the plan. The big step that remains is to put all the pieces together into a usable, coherent plan or strategy. The teacher's manual for our class presents plans for the lessons. Many times these plans do not fit the situations of particular classes, however, and must be adapted and tailored to fit our situation. As we work with the teacher's manuals; plan for our specific situations; add our own insights, interests, and skills; and devise a plan that is workable for us, we are taking the big step of developing a strategy that pulls all the pieces together.

To me, the word *strategy* suggests intentional planning. Developing a strategy implies that we know what we want to accomplish, know the steps to take, have many resources available, and are able to take charge of all the elements that contribute to an effective plan. When we as teachers assume our rightful responsibility for developing the strategy we will use with our students, it is much more likely we will gain a measure of success and satisfaction in our teaching. When we try to use someone else's (the curriculum author's) lesson plan, it may not feel like it is our plan. And when the plan doesn't work, as is occasionally the case, we are likely to blame the curriculum. It should not be surprising that someone else's plan does not work for us all the time because there are so many other factors that influence the success of a lesson that the author could not anticipate in our situation.

There are several factors that influence the success of our teaching and the effectiveness of a lesson plan.

Time. The amount of time we have influences the number and the type of activities we will provide. Involving students in activities of exploring and creating takes much more time than activities where the teacher does most of the presenting of information.

Students. The number of students we have influences our strategy. If there is one teacher to four or five students, the strategy is quite different than if a teacher is trying to work with and relate to fifteen to twenty students.

Not only the number of students, but the interests, needs, skills, and behaviors of the students affect what types of activities and resources we will include in our strategy.

Space. Factors related to the space in which the class meets include:

—the size of the room
—the way in which the room is furnished
—whether or not the room is used by other groups
—whether or not the room can be darkened
—the decorations on the walls
—whether or not floors are carpeted
—the soundproofing of walls or partitions

Teachers have very little control over these elements, but each one affects the strategy that will be developed for the class week by week.

Equipment and Resources. If the teacher's manual suggests using a filmstrip and no projector is available, then adjustments must be made in the plan. Painting activities may be recommended, but the materials necessary for painting may not be available. Bibles, Bible study tools, and other resource books are necessary if students are going to be involved in exploring activities. If such resources are not available, then adjustments must be made in the strategy. Whether or not a church has a copy machine, a spirit duplicator, a laminating machine, a paper cutter, or a videocassette recorder and camera will influence to some extent one's strategy for teaching.

Abilities and Interests. If the teacher's manual suggests using an activity (such as puppetry or role play) with which the teacher and students feel uncomfortable because of their lack of confidence or experience, it may be necessary to adapt the lesson plan. The abilities and interests of the teachers and the students influence to a significant degree the success of a lesson, and there are times when adjustments need to be made to accommodate those abilities and interests.

Season of the Year. There is quite a difference between teaching in September and in May. If it is Christmas or Easter, there will usually be more students present. Birthdays, school vacations, holidays, winter, and spring are all examples of "seasons" of the year that influence a teacher's strategy for a given session.

These six factors must be considered seriously when planning for teaching. They all influence to a significant extent our strategy for approaching a particular topic with our particular students. There is not much we can do to change the factors of time, students, space, equipment, interests, or the season of the year. However, there is quite a lot we can do to adapt and adjust the suggestions in the teacher's manual as we develop our strategies for teaching.

After we have worked with our teacher's manual and determined the main idea, the objectives, the activities, and the resources that are appropriate for a particular session, the last step in the planning process is to determine our overall strategy. There are many ways to structure a lesson plan or devise a teaching strategy. What follows is one way that I have found helpful for me in my planning for teaching. There are five identifiable parts to this strategy that I use. The five parts of the teaching strategy are presented in a logical sequence. However, in my actual week-by-week planning there are some sessions where I leave out one part in order to emphasize another part. There are also times when I rearrange the parts or include one part two or more times throughout the session. The point I am attempting to make is that even though these five parts of a lesson plan are presented in a highly structured way, it is very important to remain flexible and adaptable in order to incorporate the five parts in ways that are appropriate for a given session.

OPENING the Session, the Subject, and the Person

The first five to ten minutes of the session are very

important for setting the stage for all that will follow. In these few minutes students are deciding for themselves whether or not they want to invest themselves in what has been planned for them.

Opening activities may be any of the following:
—Welcoming each person and relating to each one individually.
—Suggesting the main idea to be studied in the session with some clues as to what other activities are planned.
—Encouraging persons to identify their own experiences, feelings, values, and ideas that are related to the main idea.
—Posing an intriguing problem, situation, or issue.
—Viewing a photograph, painting, cartoon, drawing, or poster and listing observations or raising questions.
—Brainstorming ideas, concepts, solutions, and topics to develop a resource with which to work further.
—Reading or listening to a selection of Scripture, song, speech, story, drama, or article to use as a basis for further exploration.
—Introducing an event, person, issue, or topic from a current newspaper, TV show, or magazine with which the students are familiar.
—Offering students a variety of Scripture passages, questions, or topics from which they choose one to work on with a small group or individually.
—Reading and then ranking in the order of priority a list of three to six items related to the topic of the session.

PRESENTING the Subject

After the stage is set, the next step is for teachers to provide the information about the subject of the session. Sometimes the information is presented in the form of a brief lecture. Other times the presenting aspect of the session may be describing the context in which the subject is understood, identifying the issues to be explored, stating questions that provide the focus for further investigation, or giving directions to guide exploring or creating activities.

Students may be motivated and enthused as a result of the opening, but more is needed in terms of providing information and establishing a frame of reference so that the students will have sufficient background in order to participate actively in the next three parts of the lesson.

The presenting part of the lesson can be accomplished in many ways using a variety of activities and resources,

such as the following:
—Teacher, guest, or student makes a verbal presentation that is prepared ahead of time.
—Teacher reads Scripture or story aloud as students listen.
—Teacher conducts an interview of a guest, a panel of students, or an imaginary biblical character portrayed by a student or another teacher.
—Students view and listen to film, filmstrip, or videotape that presents information in an audiovisual format.
—Teacher tells a story in a dramatic way.
—Teacher and/or students present a dramatic reading or an informal dramatization.
—Students listen to a cassette tape or a phonograph record.
—Students read from Bible, resource book, workbook, or other printed material.
—Teacher gives directions to students for an activity that will involve them in exploring the subject further.
—Teacher states questions or describes issues that will serve as a basis for further exploration.

EXPLORING the Subject

In exploring activities the students are involved in activities that call upon them to research, think, analyze, and interpret. Exploring activities can be accomplished individually, in small groups, or as a total class. As students engage in exploring activities, they become much more familiar with the subject of their study; the subject belongs to them instead of being the property of the teacher. Students move from being passive participants to becoming active participants when they engage in exploring activities. This may be the most important of the five parts of a lesson and usually will require more time than the other parts.

The role of the teacher in exploring activities is to provide clear, helpful directions, to make resources available for students to use, to offer support and encouragement as necessary, and to keep track of the progress of all the students. Teachers should resist all temptations to do the exploring for the students. The students will gain much more and will be more motivated when they are able to do the work for themselves. There are a multitude of exploring activities that can be utilized by teachers in their teaching plan. Some examples follow:
—Worksheets with directions for several steps can serve as a basis for guiding student exploration.
—Learning centers can be designed to include directions for using particular resources to explore a subject.
—Using Bibles and Bible dictionaries, concordances, commentaries, and atlases to search for information, illustrations, or interpretations is an excellent exploring activity.
—Writing reports, scripts, narratives, or articles are ways to summarize and express the subject to be explored.
—Simulation activities in which students identify with particular situations, groups, or persons and interact with others is an effective way to explore a topic.
—Preparing and/or responding to case studies is another productive way to think through a situation or issue.
—Discussions which employ analytical, open-ended questions enable students to reflect on and express their understanding and interpretations.
—Interviews where students have formed the questions and conduct the interview are another way to explore a subject.
—Debates are an excellent exploring activity, when two sides of an issue are represented by informed, enthusiastic advocates.
—Role plays involving two or more persons who identify with real or imaginary persons and situations also enable students to work through a subject that is important to them.

RESPONDING Creatively to the Subject

Learnings are reinforced and personalized when students are given the opportunity to express themselves creatively in terms of what they think, feel, and believe. Through creative expression learners are nurtured cognitively as well as affectively. Students could remain passive in the presenting part of the lesson. In the exploring part of the lesson the students become much more involved in the process. However, the subject might still be distant and abstract without affecting the students in any personal way. As they plan for activities that encourage the students to respond creatively, teachers provide the opportunities for students to relate their own personal thoughts, feelings, values, and beliefs to the subject. This part of the lesson plan is just as important for adults as it is for children and youth. Adults are accustomed to letting the teacher do all the work of presenting the lesson, although they may participate in some discussion. I have not seen very many adult classes where the adults were invited on a regular basis to express their ideas, feelings, values, and beliefs in creative ways.

Creativity can be expressed through writing and speaking as well as through painting, constructing, and dramatizing.

It would take a syllabus of many, many pages to list all of the possible activities and resources that teachers and students can use to respond creatively to the subject they are studying. Some activities to consider include:
—Writing activities (letters, poems, prayers, reports, dialogues, scripts, narratives, articles, statements of belief).
—Speaking activities (discussions, conversations, dialogues, brief presentations, statements of belief, and prayers).
—Recording activities (scripts, songs, news reports, interviews, dramas, and dialogues).
—Drama activities (role plays, puppets, informal dramatizations, pantomimes, dance, and movement).
—Constructing activities (scale models, maps, three-dimensional objects, mosaics, and clay sculpturing).
—Painting and drawing activities (tempera paint, watercolors, charcoal, felt pens, and crayons).
—Display activities (banners, posters, charts, bulletin boards, and photographs).
—Collage activities (felt, burlap, natural materials, junk, magazine pictures, and headlines).
—Photographic activities (slides, photographs, instant picture camera, and 8mm films).
—Video activities (dramatizations, interviews, how-to-do-it presentations, and travelogues).

Teacher's manuals ordinarily provide a lot of suggestions for creative activities. There are many other resource books available that provide descriptions and directions for these types of creative activities.

When we consider this part of the lesson plan, it is important to keep in mind the differences between creative activities, craft activities, and reinforcement activities.

Reinforcement activities emphasize the content of the subject and involve students in doing things that show they remember the information that was presented to them. Crossword puzzles, fill-in-the-blanks, find-the-words, connect-the-dots, and matching exercises are all examples of reinforcement activities. These are very useful activities, but they do not call forth much creativity from the students.

Craft activities usually involve materials, patterns, recipes, specific procedures, and usually have in mind a particular finished product. These are also very useful activities, but they do not encourage participants to express their own thoughts, feelings, values, and beliefs in unique, personal, creative ways.

Creative activities do not presume right answers or similar finished products. Students begin with blank sheets of paper, formless hunks of clay, or unstructured periods of time and use the available resources to express in their own original ways what they want to share with someone else.

CLOSING the Subject or the Session

We should be as intentional in planning for the closing of the session as we are for the other four parts of the lesson. Too often the closing just happens because we have run out of time, a bell or buzzer has sounded, or the parents are at the door to pick up the children. The closing of the session may be as brief as a minute or as long as ten minutes depending on the time available and the activity that is planned. There are a variety of ways to bring closure to the session:
—Students share with one another what they have created.
—Students complete brief endings to an unfinished, open-ended statement focused on the topic of the lesson.
—Students share in a litany they have written earlier.
—Teacher offers a brief prayer and/or invites students to share sentence prayers.
—Teacher leads students in singing a hymn or song that expresses the subject they have studied.
—Teacher and students recite/read together a portion of a creed, a brief statement of faith, or a passage of Scripture.
—Whole class spends one minute in silent meditation to reflect on what they have studied and how they will put their learnings into action.
—Teacher presents a brief summary of the learnings gained during the session.
—Students share brief summary statements of what they have learned during the session.
—Students and teacher listen to a recording of a song, hymn, or other musical selection; a brief story; a passage of Scripture; a portion of a sermon, or some other recorded message that adds to an understanding of the subject.

PART 2

Practicing the Planning Process

Introduction

In Part One we focused on a planning process that involves teachers in responding to four important questions, or taking four necessary steps. It is possible that Part One is sufficient in and of itself with all the information, suggestions, and examples related to:

What will we teach? .... Main Ideas

What will the learners accomplish? .... Objectives

What activities and resources
 will we plan? .... Activities and Resources

What will be our overall
 strategy? .... Teaching Strategy

However, there is something missing if we want to move from information to implementation. If there is a way for us to practice the planning process as it is described in Part One, then we will become better equipped actually to apply what we have explored to our own planning for teaching.

About fifteen years ago I published a resource that was called "The Planning Game." After using and dis-

tributing that resource for five years, I revised and expanded it. The revised edition was available for a number of years and has been out-of-print now for a few years.

"The Planning Game" included a thirty-page manual and four sets of eighty cards. Each set of cards dealt with four different topics. Using "The Planning Game" involved participants in selecting main idea cards for a unit of lessons. Then cards with objectives, activities, and resources were selected to develop the main idea. As teachers worked with the cards in small groups, they began to gain a sense of what was involved in planning for teaching. They were able to apply a similar process to their own teacher's manual.

Part One is a further revision and expansion of the original manual for "The Planning Game." However, it is so different from the original that I have decided that the whole book needs a new title.

Part Two includes four major sections including directions for using the planning cards and three different sets of planning cards. In order to use the planning cards, you *must* read and become familiar with the directions!

Directions for Using the Planning Cards

In the three sections that follow you will find three different sets of planning cards. The three sets are intended to be representative of subjects that would be appropriate for teaching three different age groups.

1. My Family, My Friends,
   and Me .... for teachers of
                                preschool through
                                third grade

2. Parables of Jesus .... for teachers of older
                                primary children,
                                youth, and adults.

3. Acts of the Apostles .... for teachers of older
                                youth and adults.

Each set includes three categories of cards: (1) Main Ideas, (2) Objectives, and (3) Activities and Resources. Each card in each set is identified by subject, category, and number. These identification marks will be helpful in sorting out the cards if two or more sets become mixed together. There are seven pages with eight cards per page for each of the three subjects. The fifty-six cards include sixteen main idea cards, sixteen objective cards, and twenty-four activities and resources cards.

Notice that there is one blank card in each category. These blank cards are for your own ideas of what should be included in the session. Make additional blank cards if they are needed.

Making the Planning Cards

The planning cards are printed in such a way that they cannot be used easily as they appear in the book. It is necessary to use a copy machine to reproduce the set(s) of planning cards that you want to use. I would suggest that you use three different colors of paper in making the cards. Use one color for the main idea cards, another color for the objective cards and a third color for the activity and resource cards. When copying the cards from the book, *print on one side only*. After printing, use scissors or a paper cutter and cut along the lines that separate the cards on each page. Assemble packs of planning cards by grouping each of the categories together. The numbers on the cards do not indicate any correct sequence. The numbers are there to identify the set of cards and to help you know if any are missing from the pack. When you finish you should have three packs of planning cards, each pack containing fifty-six cards in three colors. Each teacher or team of teachers of a particular age group will need one pack of planning cards with which to work.

Preparing to Use the Planning Cards

There are several settings in which the planning cards can be used to experience the planning process. One is for you, the reader, to go through the following process by yourself. Another is for you to meet with your team of teachers and experience the planning process together. In some instances a church educator may want to spend time during several teachers' meetings to review and discuss the four steps of the planning process. Another possibility would be to have a two- or three-hour workshop in which the four steps of planning are presented and time is provided to work with the planning cards. The workshop approach, with all the teachers from your church in attendance, is a most effective way to experience the planning process.

Before you use the planning cards it is essential that those persons using the cards understand what is meant by main ideas, objectives, activities, and resources. If you have not already done so, read the four chapters of

Part One in order to gain this background knowledge before proceeding further.

Using the Planning Cards

Follow these steps for using the cards.

Step One

Join with one or two other persons to work together. Much more is gained when two or three work as a team. As a team, select one of the three sets of planning cards that is most appropriate for the age group you teach. If you teach children, preschool through third grade, the set most appropriate for you is "My Family, My Friends, and Me." If you teach older elementary children or younger adolescents, the "Parables of Jesus" set is most appropriate for you. If you teach older adolescents or adults, you could use either "The Acts of the Apostles" or the "Parables of Jesus."

Step Two

Start with the "Main Idea" cards. Each card represents a main idea that could be the focus for part of a session, for a whole session, or for two or more sessions.

Arrange all the Main Idea cards on a table in front of you. Imagine that you are planning for a three-session unit. Review all the cards. Now select the Main Idea cards that would be appropriate for your students for each of the three sessions. Do not try to use too many of the Main Idea cards.

Arrange the Main Idea cards in the sequence they will be developed during the unit. Some sessions may have only one Main Idea card; others may have two or three cards.

As you complete this step, you should have in front of you only those Main Idea cards that you want to include in the three sessions of this unit of study. Set aside all the cards you do not plan to use.

Step Three

Display all the "Objective" cards. Read through all the cards to select those objectives that are appropriate for the main ideas you selected as well as appropriate for the ages, abilities, and interest of your particular students. You may select one or more objectives for each main idea or one objective may relate to two or three main ideas.

If you see an objective that you would like the students to accomplish but you do not have a main idea that matches it, then write out a main idea or look through the pack of discarded cards to see if there is one you could use.

It is important to remember from chapter 2 that there are different levels of objectives. As you select objectives, be sure to include several different levels in the course of the three sessions.

After selecting the Objective cards you want, lay them alongside the matching Main Idea cards. Set aside the Objective cards that you decide not to use.

Step Four

Now you are ready to use the "Activity and Resource" cards. Lay out all the cards on the table. Look over all of them to see which ones you would like to use to communicate the main idea and to help the students accomplish the objectives. As you select Activity and Resource cards, it is important to remember the ten different types or categories of activities and resources that were outlined in chapter 3. Be sure to select activities and resources that represent various types. Also, in chapter 4 we developed a teaching strategy that included five different parts of a lesson plan. Be sure to select activities that are representative of each of the five parts of a lesson.

In chapter 4 there are ten different, briefly described examples for each of the five parts of a lesson. And, there are other examples of activities and resources in chapter 3. You may want to adapt some of these suggestions and write your own cards.

Step Five

You have in front of you Main Idea and Objective cards organized in sequence for three sessions of a unit. Now arrange the Activity and Resource cards so that they are directly related to the main ideas and objectives. Be sure to select or create at least one card for each of the five parts of the lesson for each of the three sessions.

Step Six

You now have in front of you an outline of lesson plans for three class sessions. If you were actually going to teach these sessions, you would want to transfer your plans onto a lesson plan worksheet. When you have planned your curriculum, selected your main ideas, written your objectives, and chosen the activities and resources you want to use, you are ready to transfer those plans onto a lesson plan worksheet. On the next page you will find a sample lesson plan worksheet. It has been printed here on two pages so that there is enough space to hold all the notes you will need for each lesson. This worksheet may be copied on a copy machine. You may want to make a number of copies to have available as you plan your lessons throughout the year.

PLANNING WORKSHEET

Date _____   Time available _____

Unit Title _____

Session Title _____

Key Bible passage(s) _____

_____

_____

_____

Main Idea: In this session I would like to share with the students the meaning of:

_____

_____

_____

_____

_____

_____

Objectives: At the end of the session the students should be able to:

1. _____

2. _____

3. _____

4. _____

Time	Activity	Resources
	Opening:	
	Presenting:	
	Exploring:	
	Responding:	
	Closing:	

Step Seven

This step is a time of evaluation. Following are some criteria you can use to evaluate the work you have done with the planning cards.

Are the main ideas limited in number?

One of the important aspects of planning for teaching is to limit the amount of content that is expected to be presented in one session or unit. It is more important to uncover something significant than it is to try to cover all the material. If you have more than two or three Main Idea cards for each session, you are probably attempting to do too much.

Are the main ideas interrelated?

A unit of study revolves around the main ideas to be communicated to the students. These main ideas should be related to each other and presented in a coherent sequence so that they make sense to the student. Main ideas can be organized chronologically, thematically, or in some other manner.

Are the main ideas and objectives appropriate to the age groups?

Consider the age groups: their vocabulary and skills, their previous experience, and what they will experience later. Select appropriate main ideas and objectives.

Which types of teaching activities and resources are to be used?

In looking at all of the teaching activities and resources, you need to know which of the ten categories they represent. There should be a balance between the various types, with emphasis in the direction of contrived and direct experiences. If there is a heavy use of only verbal and visual activities, then learning will be less effective with minimum student motivation.

Are there a variety of activities and resources for each session?

It is important to have a variety of activities and resources so that students can make choices of what they want to do and in order to provide a change of pace during the session. Each student should be involved in more than one activity during a session.

Do the activities and resources provide for maximum student involvement and creativity?

When selecting activities and resources, choose those which encourage students to become involved in the process and which elicit from them creative responses that express their interpretations of the key concepts.

Does the overall plan reflect something that is significant to you, that you would enjoy doing?

If what you plan is not important, then it is not worth teaching. Also, if you are not going to enjoy it, the students are not likely to be interested either. The enthusiasm of the teacher is often contagious.

Have you considered more than one way to organize the unit or series of sessions?

Most teachers plan a series of sessions each with a different focus, with the whole class involved in the same process. A diagram of this type of plan is:

Another way to organize the unit is to start off by introducing all the material, then organizing the students into smaller groups to focus on one area for a week or two, and then putting it all together for a last session of summary or review. This model of organizing a unit might be diagrammed as follows:

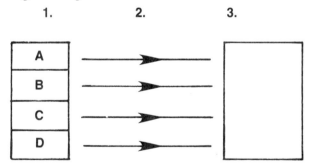

There are other ways to organize a unit. Most teachers will find themselves using one way most of the time. It would help increase the interest of students and teachers if other ways were used occasionally.

The same planning process could be used to develop a series of learning centers to implement a set of objectives for a unit of study. Each learning center should focus on a main idea and aim toward achieving an objective or two.

Have you considered how much time may be involved in each teaching activity?

Be realistic about time. Allow enough time for students to work at their own pace. Be flexible enough to adjust the schedule, if necessary. Also consider some other possibilities for the students who work quickly or have greater ability.

Implementing the Planning Cards Process

After you work with a set of planning cards, it is important to consider how this same process of planning could be applied to the week-by-week responsibility for planning church school sessions. Teachers who have used the planning cards have found a number of ways to relate the process to their usual planning for teaching.

No matter what curriculum you are using, you will find included in the teacher's manuals main ideas, objectives, activities, resources, and lesson plans or strategies. They may not be identified by the same names, but they are there either explicitly or implicitly. So, the first step for implementing the process is to translate the categories we have identified in this book into the terms used to state them in your own curriculum.

Some teachers have purchased blank 3-by-5 cards in three colors from a stationery store. As they read their teachers' manuals, they write main ideas on a card of one color, objectives on another, and activities and resources on a card of a third color. They add their own ideas to the three categories of cards. After preparing the cards, they use them in the same way we have used them in the directions described earlier. Some of these teachers have developed a filing system to keep track of the activities and resources so that the cards can be referred to at another time. They write comments on the cards noting the time required, student responses, and other things that will help them to decide whether or not to use them again.

One teacher of youth prepared several sets of cards related to a unit she was teaching about the Old Testament prophets. Instead of using the cards herself, she gave the sets of cards to small groups of students and involved them in planning the next unit of study. Not only did the students suggest some interesting ideas and helpful ways to approach the subject matter, but also showed more motivation than usual to participate in the class sessions when they studied the prophets.

Other teachers have purchased pens with three different transparent colors to mark or circle in their teachers' manuals the places where main ideas, objectives, activities, and resources were stated. After identifying all the items in each category, they made selections of the ones to use in their lesson plans and wrote them out on their planning worksheets.

The process involved in using the planning cards simulates or illustrates some very important factors involved in planning for teaching. Among these factors are:

Team Planning. Planning is more effective when two or three persons work together and collaborate with their various ideas, experiences, and resources.

Being Selective. One cannot teach everything that is important for a given session. It is necessary to be selective in order to focus on a subject and uncover what is important for that session.

Variety of Structures. There are many ways to organize subject matter for teaching. By arranging and rearranging the cards, you will come to see that there are a variety of ways to structure a session or a unit. This is especially apparent when comparing the plans of two or more groups of teachers who have worked on the same subject.

Teacher Creativity. The presence of blank cards in each of the three categories is intended to help teachers realize there is considerable latitude for them to add their own ideas, interests, experiences, and resources.

A Specific Process. By starting with main ideas, moving next to objectives, then selecting activities and resources, and culminating in a plan or strategy, we are able to work in a helpful, logical sequence.

Curriculum Materials. The packs of fifty-six cards simulate in a creative way the reality of curriculum materials. Even though teachers' manuals are published in a structured, bound format with everything presented in a clear-cut form, it is possible to arrange and rearrange the content of those pages in different ways.

MY FAMILY, MY FRIENDS, AND ME

The following set of cards may be used by teachers of preschool through third grade children.
See the directions for using the planning cards before proceeding to prepare or use the following sets of cards.

MY FAMILY, MY FRIENDS, AND ME

Main Idea

Friends are important persons for young children. Friends are persons who are fun to be with, who enjoy some of the same things you enjoy, and who care about you.

M1

MY FAMILY, MY FRIENDS, AND ME

Main Idea

Young children have friends in their neighborhood, in the church school, and in the preschool they attend. It is fun to be a friend: to share games and toys, to play together, and to share conversations.

M2

MY FAMILY, MY FRIENDS, AND ME

Main Idea

Jesus had many friends. Jesus shared meals, stories, trips, and other experiences with his friends. Jesus showed his friends how to be loving, caring, and helpful to others, even their enemies.

M3

MY FAMILY, MY FRIENDS, AND ME

Main Idea

Children belong to a family. Many different persons make up a family: mothers, fathers, brothers, sisters, cousins, aunts, uncles, grandparents, and others.

M4

MY FAMILY, MY FRIENDS, AND ME

Main Idea

Families share happy and sad experiences together. Special meals, celebrations, trips, parties, games, picnics, stories, and prayers are happy experiences. Illnesses, arguments, disappointments, accidents, deaths, divorces, and punishments are sad experiences. In both happy and sad experiences God is with us to help us to learn and grow.

M5

MY FAMILY, MY FRIENDS, AND ME

Main Idea

With families and friends persons experience many different kinds of feelings for others and for themselves at various times: love, trust, forgiveness, jealousy, anger, fear, sadness, happiness, thankfulness, joy, loneliness, and other feelings as well.

M6

MY FAMILY, MY FRIENDS, AND ME

Main Idea

Children can be sensitive to the feelings and thoughts of members of their families and their friends. Children can communicate their thoughts and feelings to others by the words they speak as well as by the expressions of their hands, eyes, face, and whole body.

M7

MY FAMILY, MY FRIENDS, AND ME

Main Idea

There are many children in the world. Most children live in families. Families around the world have different customs and values. God plans for everyone to belong to a family.

M8

MY FAMILY, MY FRIENDS, AND ME

Main Idea

Everything and everyone in the world has a name. Names are important. Some names have special meanings. When we know persons' names, we know something special about them. We should learn people's names and call them by name.

M9

MY FAMILY, MY FRIENDS, AND ME

Main Idea

Sometimes children have good feelings and sometimes they have bad feelings. It is important to learn what causes feelings and how feelings can change. It is also important to believe that God loves us, and so do our parents, no matter what feelings we have.

M10

MY FAMILY, MY FRIENDS, AND ME

Main Idea

God plans for all living things (plants, animals, and people) to be born, to grow, and to die. Children can help God by caring for living things and helping them grow.

M11

MY FAMILY, MY FRIENDS, AND ME

Main Idea

God has created us to have bodies with hands, feet, eyes, ears, nose, mouth, and a brain. Feet can go lots of places and do lots of things. Hands can be used in many ways. Eyes can see many things. Ears can hear many sounds. A nose can smell many odors, and a mouth can taste many flavors.

M12

MY FAMILY, MY FRIENDS, AND ME

Main Idea

Some children in our community and world are hungry, cannot see or hear, do not have strong arms or legs, have sick bodies, or do not have families that love them. These children need lots of help and love. God loves and helps them. Nurses and doctors love and help them. We can love and help some children that we know.

M13

MY FAMILY, MY FRIENDS, AND ME

Main Idea

Children can express their love and thankfulness to God for their family, friends, and themselves by saying prayers and singing songs. Children can also speak words of thankfulness to their family and friends.

M14

MY FAMILY, MY FRIENDS, AND ME

Main Idea

In the Bible there are many stories about families and friends. We can read and hear Bible stories to learn about what kinds of relationships God wishes for families and friends to have with each other.

M15

MY FAMILY, MY FRIENDS, AND ME

Main Idea

(Write your own)

M16

MY FAMILY, MY FRIENDS, AND ME

Objective

The children will be enabled to:

recall some ways they need other persons and ways other persons need them;

suggest some ways to be helpful to persons in their family and to friends;

act in a helpful way to someone else.

M17

MY FAMILY, MY FRIENDS, AND ME

Objective

The children will be enabled to:

name all the persons who belong to their family;

describe their relationship to each person in their family;

explain in their own words what they think is important about a family and belonging to a family.

M18

MY FAMILY, MY FRIENDS, AND ME

Objective

The children will be enabled to:

name persons who are their friends;

suggest some feelings and actions that are important in a friendship;

plan to do something with a friend.

M19

MY FAMILY, MY FRIENDS, AND ME

Objective

The children will be enabled to:

discuss some thoughts and feelings they have about God, about their families, about their friends, and about themselves;

describe feelings they have related to happy and sad experiences.

M20

MY FAMILY, MY FRIENDS, AND ME

Objective

The children will be enabled to:

state some of the feelings they had that day or recently;

express in a nonverbal way some of the feelings they mentioned so that another person will understand those feelings;

use a creative form to express some of their feelings.

M21

MY FAMILY, MY FRIENDS, AND ME

Objective

The children will be enabled to:

retell in their own words one of the stories about Jesus and his friends;

relate in some way the story about Jesus to their own experiences of friends and friendship.

M22

MY FAMILY, MY FRIENDS, AND ME

Objective

The children will be enabled to:

compare pictures of persons in families from different parts of the world;

describe some of the differences and similarities about those persons;

relate some of the differences and similarities to their own families.

M23

MY FAMILY, MY FRIENDS, AND ME

Objective

The children will be enabled to:

identify by name many different objects in the room and in photographs;

identify all the other children in the class by name;

identify their teacher(s) by name;

tell something special about their own name.

M24

MY FAMILY, MY FRIENDS, AND ME

Objective

The children will be enabled to:

name feelings they have had;
describe whether the feelings were happy or sad;
explain what they think might cause their feelings;
suggest some ways that feelings can change.

M25

MY FAMILY, MY FRIENDS, AND ME

Objective

The children will be enabled to:

talk about the way living things are born, grow, and die;
share some feelings they have about birth, growth, and death;
observe that birth, growth, and death are normal occurrences in nature and in personal life.

M26

MY FAMILY, MY FRIENDS, AND ME

Objective

The children will be enabled to:

compare the differences between babies and grownups of several species;
arrange in correct order pictures which show different stages of growth of several species;
illustrate in a creative way their own understanding of stages of growth.

M27

MY FAMILY, MY FRIENDS, AND ME

Objective

The children will be enabled to:

tell about some things they could not do when they were babies that they can do now;
describe some things they will be able to do when they are older that they cannot do now.

M28

MY FAMILY, MY FRIENDS, AND ME

Objective

The children will be enabled to:

say a brief prayer of thankfulness for whatever is important or special to them;
sing a song to express their thankfulness for their family and friends;
say words of thanks to their family and friends.

M29

MY FAMILY, MY FRIENDS, AND ME

Objective

The children will be enabled to:

show some of the special things their feet, hands, ears, eyes, nose, and mouth do;
use their senses to identify a wide variety of objects, sounds, odors, and tastes.

M30

MY FAMILY, MY FRIENDS, AND ME

Objective

The children will be enabled to:

describe needs (physical, emotional, and relational) of other children in their community and world;
give examples of ways persons with special skills help minister to those needs;
decide on a way to show love and caring to some person(s) in the church or community with a special need.

M31

MY FAMILY, MY FRIENDS, AND ME

Objective

The children will be enabled to:

(Write your own)

M32

MY FAMILY, MY FRIENDS, AND ME

Activity

Teacher reads or tells a story about one or more of the following topics:

—playing and sharing with friends;
—ways families live together;
—families in other cultures;
—being born, growing, and dying.

Resource(s)
Storybooks

M33

MY FAMILY, MY FRIENDS, AND ME

Activity

Teacher reads or tells a story from the Bible about family and friends, a story about Jesus' relationships with his friends, or a story about helping other persons who have special needs.

Resources(s)
Bibles, Bible storybooks

M34

MY FAMILY, MY FRIENDS, AND ME

Activity

Children make their own "books" about families by illustrating pages titled:

A Mother Is . . .   A Mother Does . . .
A Father Is . . .   A Father Does . . .
Families Are Important Because . . . .
I Am Glad I Belong To My Family Because. . . .

Resources(s)
Paper, crayons, paints, chalk, magazines, scissors, glue, etc.

M35

MY FAMILY, MY FRIENDS, AND ME

Activity

Children can participate in interest activity centers which may include:

—books and stories   —games with friends
—housekeeping   —listening to music
—dressing up   —blocks and toys
—puzzles   —conversation

Resource(s)
Materials necessary for each interest center

M36

MY FAMILY, MY FRIENDS, AND ME

Activity

Children share feelings they have about experiences with friends and family. Children select photographs to illustrate their understanding of feelings and tell brief stories about their photographs.

Resources(s)
A collection of photographs cut from magazines

M37

MY FAMILY, MY FRIENDS, AND ME

Activity

Children select photographs to illustrate happy feelings and others to illustrate sad feelings. With photographs they tell brief stories to express what causes happy and sad feelings.

Resource(s)
A collection of photographs

M38

MY FAMILY, MY FRIENDS, AND ME

Activity

Children see a filmstrip about families, friends, families in the world, Jesus and his friends, or persons in need.
Use filmstrip as a basis for conversation and personal sharing and as a stimulus for their own creative expressions.

Resources(s)
Filmstrip, projector, screen, recording of script, cassette recorder, and creative activity materials

M39

MY FAMILY, MY FRIENDS, AND ME

Activity

Teacher leads children in a game where they work at learning everyone's name in the class. Having spoken with parents ahead of time, teacher shares a brief story about each child's name.

Resource(s)
Game materials

M40

MY FAMILY, MY FRIENDS, AND ME

Activity

Children listen to one or more songs about friends and friendship. After listening to song(s), children learn song(s) to sing-a-long with recording.

Resource(s)
Record and record player or cassette and tape player

M41

MY FAMILY, MY FRIENDS, AND ME

Activity

Teachers and children take a walk around the church to find as many things as they can to hear, to smell, or to touch. When they return to the classroom, they make as long a list as possible of things they experienced.

Resource(s)
None

M42

MY FAMILY, MY FRIENDS, AND ME

Activity

Children make cookies, bread, or something else that they can experience with all their senses. They share their food among themselves and take some to share with another class.

Resource(s)
Utensils and ingredients for cooking, kitchen

M43

MY FAMILY, MY FRIENDS, AND ME

Activity

Children are guided to act out a story with puppets, pantomime, or informal dramatization to express relationships with families or friends, or to express various feelings.

Resources
Puppets, costumes, simple props

M44

MY FAMILY, MY FRIENDS, AND ME

Activity

Children learn prayers and songs to express thanksgiving to God. Children speak their own brief extemporaneous prayers of thanks. Children decide upon a way to say "thank you" to parents or friends.

Resource(s)
Prayers and songs

M45

MY FAMILY, MY FRIENDS, AND ME

Activity

Children sing a song about friends, then list ways friends help each other. Talk about ways to help at home, and ways in which parents, brothers, and sisters help at home. Discuss how it feels when someone helps you when you need help.

Resource(s)
Song

M46

MY FAMILY, MY FRIENDS, AND ME

Activity

Children draw pictures of things they can do now that they could not do when they were babies, and things they would like to be able to do when they get older.

Resources
Materials for drawing pictures

M47

MY FAMILY, MY FRIENDS, AND ME

Activity

Using drawings, illustrations, or photographs the children arrange to show in chronological order the different stages of development of a person, a plant, a dog, a tree, or something else. Teacher talks about God's plan for everything to be born, to grow, and to die.

Resource(s)
Drawings, illustrations, or photographs

M48

MY FAMILY, MY FRIENDS, AND ME

Activity

Teachers prepare a large "pie" chart with title in the center: "God Loves Me All the Time." For each "slice" children can state a feeling that the teacher can print in the "slice." Then the children select pictures that represent the feelings and paste them on the chart. For each slice or feeling a prayer can be composed to express that feeling.

Resource(s)
    A chart and pictures

M49

MY FAMILY, MY FRIENDS, AND ME

Activity

Children use puppets to tell a story they have created.

Resource(s)
    Puppets

M50

MY FAMILY, MY FRIENDS, AND ME

Activity

Children pantomime, dance, or use body movement to:
    —express feelings;
    —show what different parts of the body can do;
    —say "thank you" to God.

Resource(s)
    None

M51

MY FAMILY, MY FRIENDS, AND ME

Activity

Children select photographs that show other children with special needs. Children tell about others they know with special needs. Teacher and children discuss ways they and others can respond to some of the needs.

Resource(s)
    Photographs

M52

MY FAMILY, MY FRIENDS, AND ME

Activity

Teacher reads or tells a story about death and dying, such as *Mr. Red Ears*. Children share thoughts and feelings about death. They tell about experiences of pets, friends, or family members dying. Children act out a particular scene from the story.

Resource(s)
    An appropriate storybook

M53

MY FAMILY, MY FRIENDS, AND ME

Activity

Children listen as teacher reads *Talking Without Words* by Marie Hall Ets (A Viking Seafarer book).

Discuss how persons can send messages without words by using different parts of the body. Children can take turns "telling" the others something without using words.

Resource(s)
    The book *Talking Without Words*

M54

MY FAMILY, MY FRIENDS, AND ME

Activity

Children visit the church nursery to see the babies and they visit an adult class. They could sing a song for each class. When they return to their room, they talk about what is special about babies and grown-ups.

Resource(s)
    None

M55

MY FAMILY, MY FRIENDS, AND ME

Activity

(Devise your own)

Resource(s)

(Select resources you need)

M56

PARABLES OF JESUS

The following set of cards may be used by
teachers of children (fourth-grade and older), youth, and adults.
See the directions for using the planning cards
before proceeding to prepare or use the following sets of cards.

PARABLES OF JESUS

Main Idea

A parable is a simple story or illustration which uses familiar objects or experiences to teach a more profound religious truth. The story is comparable to an important aspect of a person's relationship with God or with other persons. Parables usually have one central purpose or meaning.

P1

PARABLES OF JESUS

Main Idea

Parables are different from fables, allegories, and myths. A *fable* is a ficticious story to teach a moral lesson, usually involving animals as the primary characters. An *allegory* is a story in which each character, object, or event represents some hidden or symbolic meaning. A *myth* is a traditional story, with some historical references, that seeks to explain the origins of natural and supernatural phenomena.

P2

PARABLES OF JESUS

Main Idea

Jesus was a remarkable teacher who taught persons in many different ways and places. One of the ways Jesus taught was with parables. Jesus used parables to teach about the many dimensions of responsible relationships between persons and with God.

P3

PARABLES OF JESUS

Main Idea

Some of the parables teach what Jesus means when he speaks of the kingdom of God or the kingdom of heaven. Included among these parables are:
—The laborers in the vineyard (Mt. 20:1-16);
—The marriage feast (Mt. 22:1-10);
—The two sons (Mt. 21:28-31);
—The mustard seed (Mt. 13:31-32);
—The wheat and the tares (Mt. 13:24-30).

P4

PARABLES OF JESUS

Main Idea

There are between forty and fifty parables recorded in the Four Gospels. The parables are of different lengths and types. They are used for a variety of purposes and are addressed to different audiences.

P5

PARABLES OF JESUS

Main Idea

The parables of Jesus focus on questions, situations, and feelings that are similar to what people experience today. The teachings of Jesus contained in his parables are relevant to the faith and life of his followers.

P6

PARABLES OF JESUS

Main Idea

In order for us to understand the meaning of a parable of Jesus, it is important to understand the setting in which it was told, the persons to whom it was addressed, and the intent Jesus seems to have for telling the parable.

P7

PARABLES OF JESUS

Main Idea

In Matthew 13, Jesus tells seven different parables. Jesus also explains why he teaches with parables and he interprets two of the parables.

P8

PARABLES OF JESUS

Main Idea

In Luke 15, there are three parables: the lost sheep, the lost coin, and the lost son. These parables teach about God's continuous seeking for those who are lost as well as the joyous celebration after finding and receiving back those who are lost.

P9

PARABLES OF JESUS

Main Idea

The parable of the lost son expresses many different feelings found in the three main characters of the story. These feelings include: love, loneliness, hunger, repentance, forgiveness, resentment, acceptance, and joy.

P10

PARABLES OF JESUS

Main Idea

The parable of the lost sheep appears in Luke 15:3-7 and Matthew 18:12-14. In Luke the parable is addressed to the Scribes and Pharisees and in Matthew it is addressed to the disciples. Consequently, the application of the parable is different in each Gospel.

P11

PARABLES OF JESUS

Main Idea

The parable of the lost son has also been called the parable of the prodigal or the parable of the loving father. This parable compares two sons and the way the father relates to both of them with love, acceptance, and forgiveness. We can identify with one or both of the sons and we can see the father as representing God.

P12

PARABLES OF JESUS

Main Idea

The parable of the good Samaritan was told by Jesus in response to the question, "Who is my neighbor?" Jesus' answer suggests that we are neighbor to everyone, even our enemies. There are persons in need of good Samaritans today and there are times when we can be good Samaritans.

P13

PARABLES OF JESUS

Main Idea

The parables of Jesus are intended to be understood and applied personally. As we read or hear the parables, we can identify personally with the characters or situations in order to relate them to our own experiences of relationships with other persons and with God.

P14

PARABLES OF JESUS

Main Idea

It is possible today to discover or create parables using familiar, contemporary experiences to communicate the meaning of one's life and faith in relationship to God and other persons.

P15

PARABLES OF JESUS

Main Idea

(Write your own)

P16

PARABLES OF JESUS

Objective

Participants will be enabled to *locate* in the Gospels all of the parables of Jesus and *place them* in several different categories.

P17

PARABLES OF JESUS

Objective

Participants will be enabled to *define* the word "parable" and *describe* the differences between parables and fables, allegories and myths.

P18

PARABLES OF JESUS

Objective

Participants will be enabled to *use* a Bible concordance, dictionary, and commentary to *locate* four to six parables dealing with the kingdom of God (or heaven) and *explain* the meaning of each.

P19

PARABLES OF JESUS

Objective

Participants will be enabled to *contrast* the similarities and differences of one parable as it is written in two or more of the Gospels.

P20

PARABLES OF JESUS

Objective

Participants will be enabled to *retell* from memory a specific selected parable and to *express* in their own words what the central meaning of that parable is.

P21

PARABLES OF JESUS

Objective

Participants will be enabled to *interpret* a parable in terms of its context, the audience to whom it was addressed, Jesus' purpose in telling it, and its central meaning.

P22

PARABLES OF JESUS

Objective

Participants will be enabled to *describe* some of the ways and places where Jesus served as a teacher and *explain* some reasons why Jesus used parables in his teaching.

P23

PARABLES OF JESUS

Objective

Participants will be enabled to *summarize* the concept of the kingdom of God (or heaven) using as illustrations several of the parables of Jesus.

P24

PARABLES OF JESUS

Objective

Participants will be enabled to *paraphrase* in their own words the story line of one or more parables and *illustrate* in a visual medium the same parables(s).

P25

PARABLES OF JESUS

Objective

Participants will be enabled to *identify* a variety of feelings that are present in a parable and *express* those feelings through a creative form.

P26

PARABLES OF JESUS

Objective

Participants will be enabled to *express* in a creative form one or more of the parables of Jesus by *illustrating* the story line and the central meaning of the parable.

P27

PARABLES OF JESUS

Objective

Participants will be enabled to *show* from their own experiences what they understand Jesus to mean in one or more of his parables.

P28

PARABLES OF JESUS

Objective

Participants will be enabled to *relate* the meaning of a parable of Jesus for his time to its meaning for our time and *decide* how to live in the light of that meaning.

P29

PARABLES OF JESUS

Objective

Participants will be enabled to *help* others in their group, family, or church to understand the meaning of one or more parables of Jesus by *interpreting* the parable in ways that *apply* to their own lives.

P30

PARABLES OF JESUS

Objective

Participants will be enabled to *create* a parable using contemporary objects and experiences and *apply* that parable to their own life situation.

P31

PARABLES OF JESUS

Objective

Participants will be enabled to . . . .

(Write your own)

P32

PARABLES OF JESUS

Activity

Teacher provides directions to guide students to use resource books so they can find definitions of parables, fables, allegories, and myths.

Resource(s)

Dictionaries, word books, etc.

P33

PARABLES OF JESUS

Activity

Teacher presents the story of a parable by:
— telling the story;
— showing a filmstrip;
— playing a tape recording.

Resource(s)

Filmstrip, projector, screen, cassette, and recorder

P34

PARABLES OF JESUS

Activity

Teacher, guest speaker, or prepared participant presents a brief lecture about Jesus' use of parables, characteristics of a parable, and ways of interpreting parables.

Resource(s)

Chalkboard or newsprint, chalk or felt-tipped pens, guest speaker

P35

PARABLES OF JESUS

Activity

Students prepare ahead of time to present one or more parables through the use of puppets, an informal dramatization, or a readers' theater format.

Resource(s)

Puppets, costumes, scripts

P36

PARABLES OF JESUS

Activity

After sharing a parable, the teacher invites participants to share their own questions about the setting, purpose, or meaning of the parable. The questions are written down to use as a reference for further exploration.

Resource(s)

Chalkboard or newsprint, chalk or felt-tipped pens

P37

PARABLES OF JESUS

Activity

The teacher and participants spend time together considering familiar stories, cartoons, photographs, or poems that appear to "say" one thing but contain a second or hidden meaning.

Resource(s)

Stories, cartoons, photographs, poems

P38

PARABLES OF JESUS

Activity

Teacher arranges in advance and provides directions for several learning centers for the purpose of:
— viewing a filmstrip;
— listening to a recording;
— reading parable(s) in several translations;
— reading Bible resource books.

Resource(s)

Filmstrip, recording, Bibles, resource books, projector, screen, record or cassette player

P39

PARABLES OF JESUS

Activity

Participants use Bibles and resource books for locating all the parables of Jesus and for organizing the parables in as many categories as are appropriate.

Resource(s)

Bibles, resource books

P40

PARABLES OF JESUS

Activity

Teacher guides participants in their study of a parable to:
—identify its setting and purpose;
—discuss its meaning;
—relate its meaning to their own faith and life.

Resource(s)
Bibles, resource books

P41

PARABLES OF JESUS

Activity

Participants use Bible study resources to work at their own understandings and interpretations of one or more parables. Where parables appear in more than one Gospel, they seek to identify similarities and differences between them.

Resource(s)
Bibles, resource books

P42

PARABLES OF JESUS

Activity

Participants work in small groups, each group with a different parable. In their groups they will read the parable, consult available resources, and discuss their interpretations. They will become familiar enough with the parable to tell it to another person from memory.

Resource(s)
Bibles, resource books

P43

PARABLES OF JESUS

Activity

Using a filmstrip of a parable, the participants will work in two groups. Group 1 will use the *script* as a basis for creating their own slides or transparencies. Group 2 will use the *filmstrip* itself as a basis for writing their own script.

Resource(s)
Filmstrip, projector, screen, slides, pens, paper, slide projector

P44

PARABLES OF JESUS

Activity

Each participant will select one parable to read and study in order to write a paraphrase of that parable. Or, they create their own parable with contemporary characters and objects to express the same meaning as the parable that Jesus told.

Resource(s)
Bibles, resource books, paper, pencils

P45

PARABLES OF JESUS

Activity

Teacher guides participants in playing a game, or some other fun activity, that will help them to learn the names and stories of a variety of the parables.

Resource(s)
Game materials

P46

PARABLES OF JESUS

Activity

Teacher and participants take a walk in the neighborhood near the church to look for examples from nature, people, buildings, or other objects which may provide content for creating contemporary parables.

Resource(s)
The neighborhood

P47

PARABLES OF JESUS

Activity

Participants work individually or in small groups to:
—create puppets;
—select slides or photographs;
—create slides or transparencies;
—produce a recording;
of one parable in order to share it with others.

Resource(s)
Puppets, slides, photographs, transparencies, blank cassette, projectors, recorder

P48

PARABLES OF JESUS

Activity

Participants create puppets and write a script in order to interpret their understanding of the meaning of a parable and then share their puppet show with the whole class.

Resource(s)
   Materials to make puppets

P49

PARABLES OF JESUS

Activity

Participants work in small groups, each group with a different parable. Each group decides on a way to present and interpret the parable through role play, dramatization, or other means.

Resource(s)
   None

P50

PARABLES OF JESUS

Activity

Participants will relate the parable of the good Samaritan to contemporary life by giving examples they know of, discussing the implications of being a good Samaritan, and describing who some of the "wounded" are today who need help.

Resource(s)
   None

P51

PARABLES OF JESUS

Activity

Participants will prepare to tell a parable and then go to another class in the church school to share their parable with that class.

Resource(s)
   None

P52

PARABLES OF JESUS

Activity

Participants will use a tape recorder in order to record:
   —a reading of a parable;
   —a creative paraphrase of a parable;
   —the telling of a contemporary parable.

Resource(s)
   Blank tape, cassette recorder

P53

PARABLES OF JESUS

Activity

Participants will write a creative dialogue between themselves and one of the characters of a parable.

Resource(s)
   Paper, pencil

P54

PARABLES OF JESUS

Activity

Teacher guides participants in discussion of parable(s) in order to relate its meaning to their own faith and life experiences. Together they decide ways to apply the parable(s) to their lives.

Resource(s)
   None

P55

PARABLES OF JESUS

Activity

(Devise your own)

Resource(s)

(Select your own)

P56

ACTS OF THE APOSTLES

Teachers of youth and adults will find these cards to
be helpful and useful. Creative teachers may find that the content
can be adapted for some fifth- and sixth-grade classes.
See the directions for using the planning cards
before proceeding to prepare or use the following set of cards.

ACTS OF THE APOSTLES

Main Idea

A disciple is a person who follows and learns from someone else. Persons who followed and learned from Jesus were called disciples. Followers of Jesus were also called Christians, People of the Way, and believers.

A1

ACTS OF THE APOSTLES

Main Idea

Jesus commissioned all his followers, "Go, then, to all peoples everywhere and make them my disciples . . . baptize them . . . teach them . . . when the Holy Spirit comes you will be filled with power . . . you will be witnesses for me in Jerusalem, in all of Judea and Samaria, and to the ends of the earth" (Matthew 28:19; Acts 1:8, TEV).

A2

ACTS OF THE APOSTLES

Main Idea

Twelve of the disciples of Jesus plus Paul were identified by the special title of "apostle." The word "apostle" means "messenger." The apostles were witnesses of the risen Lord, Jesus Christ, and proclaimed the message of the risen Lord to people throughout the land.

A3

ACTS OF THE APOSTLES

Main Idea

The apostles were very enthusiastic about and committed to the work Jesus called them to do. Many times in many places they spoke and acted fearlessly in the face of great opposition and danger. Persons today are called to represent Jesus by proclaiming his good news of salvation.

A4

ACTS OF THE APOSTLES

Main Idea

The apostle Peter was a bold, faithful spokesman for God in the early days after Jesus' death and resurrection. Peter spoke on the day of Pentecost when many believed and were baptized. He healed, taught, preached, and baptized. After his vision at Joppa, Peter convinced others that the Gentiles could be baptized without first being circumcised.

A5

ACTS OF THE APOSTLES

Main Idea

A summary of the beliefs of the early church can be expressed as follows: "The prophecies of the Old Covenant have been fulfilled and a new age has begun in Jesus Christ. He was born of the seed of David, he died according to the Scriptures, he was buried, he rose on the third day, he is exalted at the right hand of God, and he will come again."

A6

ACTS OF THE APOSTLES

Main Idea

In its early days the church was led by persons with special gifts for teaching, preaching, serving, and healing. Individually or in teams these leaders contributed very much to the structure and direction of the church. Among the leaders were: Peter, John, James, Stephen, Paul, Silas, Barnabas, and Timothy.

A7

ACTS OF THE APOSTLES

Main Idea

The apostle Paul can be identified by many roles: Hebrew, Pharisee, tentmaker, Roman citizen, apostle, traveler, missionary, organizer, defender, servant, prisoner, martyr. In the book of Acts there are passages that provide background and examples of each of these significant roles.

A8

ACTS OF THE APOSTLES

Main Idea

Saul of Tarsus was a Pharisee who was committed to eliminating those who were followers of Jesus. Saul was present and assented to the killing of Stephen. On a trip to Damascus for the purpose of seeking out more followers of Jesus, Saul encountered the power and presence of the risen Christ in an experience that caused him to be blind. Saul's name became Paul. He was helped and baptized by Ananias. Paul became an outspoken, committed apostle of Jesus Christ.

A9

ACTS OF THE APOSTLES

Main Idea

In the book of Acts there are many speeches and sermons that correspond to specific settings and present the central beliefs of the early church. Among the speeches are:
—Peter speaking at Pentecost (2:14-47)
—Peter speaking in the Temple (3:12-26)
—Stephen witnessing to his faith (7:1-53)
—Peter speaking about his vision (10:34-43)
—Paul speaking in the synagogue (13:13-52)
—Paul defending himself (21:27–22:29).

A10

ACTS OF THE APOSTLES

Main Idea

Some of the important cities visited by Paul and his companions were: Antioch, Damascus, Jerusalem, Ephesus, Philippi, Corinth, Troas, Thessalonica, Caesarea, Perga, Iconium, Lystra, and Derbe. In each city there were experiences of friendship and affirmation as well as hostility and opposition.

A11

ACTS OF THE APOSTLES

Main Idea

The early church was engaged in a variety of important tasks:
—Remembering, speaking about, writing, and sharing the words and actions of Jesus
—Developing a style of worship
—Caring for the sick, poor, widowed, hungry, lonely, and oppressed persons
—Organizing and setting standards
These continue to be important tasks of the church and Christians today.

A12

ACTS OF THE APOSTLES

Main Idea

Ministry in the church and the community is the responsibility of all God's people. In our baptism we are commissioned for ministry. Leaders and members of the church have different gifts and different responsibilities that can all be used to enhance the whole ministry of the church. It is important to discern our call from God, to identify our gifts, and to respond with commitment for serving Jesus Christ and his ministry.

A13

ACTS OF THE APOSTLES

Main Idea

Creeds, confessions of faith, catechisms, constitutions, statements of belief, and hymns are all examples of ways the church has chosen to express what it believes. Such resources contain statements regarding the responsibilities of God's people for participating in and extending the ministry of Jesus Christ.

A14

ACTS OF THE APOSTLES

Main Idea

As churches and individuals, we need to discern what God's message is that must be shared with people and institutions today. We need to learn from the Scriptures, articulate our beliefs, and affirm our commitments in order to be God's messengers of peace, justice, and salvation.

A15

ACTS OF THE APOSTLES

Main Idea

(Write your own)

A16

ACTS OF THE APOSTLES

Objective

The participants will be enabled to:
write or *state* in their own words some of the characteristics of the early Christian disciples and what was expected of them in their life and work.
They will be able to
relate their description to followers of Jesus today.

A17

ACTS OF THE APOSTLES

Objective

The participants will be enabled to:
use a Bible dictionary in order to *define* the meaning of some of the following words:

disciple   gospel   Pentecost
apostle   martyr   Pharisee
Christian   baptize   resurrection
church   Holy Spirit   circumcise
(and other words you may select)

A18

ACTS OF THE APOSTLES

Objective

The participants will be enabled to:
recall ten important events in the life of the apostle Paul;
list them in chronological order;
state in their own words the significance of each event.

A19

ACTS OF THE APOSTLES

Objective

The participants will be enabled to:
identify two or three "turning point" experiences in Paul's life;
explain why those experiences were so crucial;
describe one or two "turning point" experiences in their own lives;
share with others something of the significance of those experiences.

A20

ACTS OF THE APOSTLES

Objective

The participants will be enabled to:
name six of the key persons in the book of Acts;
describe the contributions of those persons to the life and work of the early church;
relate in a personal way to one of the persons in terms of the work, message, or circumstance of that person.

A21

ACTS OF THE APOSTLES

Objective

The participants will be enabled to:
compare the experiences, concerns, and contributions of the apostles Peter and Paul;
show how some of those experiences, concerns or contributions are relevant to the church today.

A22

ACTS OF THE APOSTLES

Objective

The participants will be enabled to:
suggest at least five roles that were characteristic of Paul's life and ministry;
select a passage of Scripture that represents each role;
create a *visual, dramatize,* or *write* a personal interpretation of one of the roles.

A23

ACTS OF THE APOSTLES

Objective

The participants will be enabled to:
locate six important speeches or sermons in the book of Acts;
summarize the central message of each;
compare the similar and different emphases of each;
interpret their understanding of one of the speeches or sermons.

A24

ACTS OF THE APOSTLES

Objective

The participants will be enabled to:
summarize the gospel message of the leaders of the early church;
find in the Old Testament and the Gospels the roots of that message;
compare that message with the message of the church today.

A25

ACTS OF THE APOSTLES

Objective

The participants will be enabled to:
locate on a map some of the key cities mentioned in Acts;
describe one important event that happened in each city;
draw on a map one of the missionary journeys of Paul.

A26

ACTS OF THE APOSTLES

Objective

The participants will be enabled to:
identify some of the important tasks of the early church and its leaders;
rank those tasks in their order of importance for establishing the church;
relate the tasks of ministry in today's church to the tasks of the early church;
select a task of ministry in which to participate to help the church today.

A27

ACTS OF THE APOSTLES

Objective

The participants will be enabled to:
describe some of the conflicts and controversies that were experienced by the early Christians;
compare those with the conflicts and controversies Christians experience today in the church;
illustrate these experiences in a creative way;
suggest ways that such difficulties can be overcome.

A28

ACTS OF THE APOSTLES

Objective

The participants will be enabled to:
select some persons from contemporary history, news, or experiences who are acting in ways similar to people in the early church;
describe the similarities and differences;
interpret the significance of those actions for understanding the work of the church.

A29

ACTS OF THE APOSTLES

Objective

The participants will be enabled to:
explore church documents such as creeds, confessions, catechisms, statements of belief, and hymns in order to find expressions of what is expected of God's people regarding their ministry;
paraphrase selected statements in their own words;
write their own statements of belief.

A30

ACTS OF THE APOSTLES

Objective

The participants will be enabled to:
explain what it means to be called by God to engage in ministry;
identify their own gifts for ministry in the church and the community;
show how they personally are engaged in ministry;
decide on one or more ways they can serve in the ongoing ministry of God's people.

A31

ACTS OF THE APOSTLES

Objective

The participants will be enabled to:

(Devise some of your own objectives)

A32

ACTS OF THE APOSTLES

Activity

Use available resource books and key passages from Acts to develop definitions of key words. Each individual or small group works on a different word. After exploring definitions, participants share findings and discuss interpretations.

Resource(s)
Bibles, Bible dictionaries, word books, or other resources

A33

ACTS OF THE APOSTLES

Activity

Teacher presents information or tells stories about important events in the life and work of the apostle Peter or apostle Paul. Or, students work individually or in pairs to explore the important events in the life and work of Peter or Paul.

Resource(s)
Bibles, Bible dictionaries, atlases, commentaries, or other books about Peter or Paul.

A34

ACTS OF THE APOSTLES

Activity

Students, working individually or in small groups, select one key person in Acts and find information about the person's:
—life and work;
—relationships to others;
—beliefs about God, Jesus, etc.;
—contributions to the church.

Resource(s)
Bibles, Bible dictionaries, books about persons of the Bible, and other resources

A35

ACTS OF THE APOSTLES

Activity

Teacher leads discussion of a specific topic, text, issue, event, or person by asking questions that enable students to interpret the meaning of the subject and to apply the subject to their own faith and life experiences.

Resource(s)
Bibles

A36

ACTS OF THE APOSTLES

Activity

Teacher divides the chapters of Acts evenly among the students. The students look for all the examples of major sermons or speeches that are included in Acts. A list of speeches is made. The speeches are analyzed according to setting, persons speaking, audience, content, and reactions.

Resource(s)
Bibles

A37

ACTS OF THE APOSTLES

Activity

Students are invited to:
—give illustrations of the subject from recent or current history;
—describe something of their own feelings, values, beliefs, or experiences; or
—reflect on situations, persons, or events in their own church.

Resource(s)
None

A38

ACTS OF THE APOSTLES

Activity

Teacher and students work with maps to locate key cities mentioned in Acts, to trace one or more journeys of the apostle Paul, or to see the relation of the growth of the church to the rest of the world.

Resource(s)
Bibles, atlases, and maps

A39

ACTS OF THE APOSTLES

Activity

Teacher directs students to passages in Acts that describe conflicts between individuals, groups, and communities. Students suggest events and experiences that are illustrative of the difficulties present in the world and church today.

Resource(s)
Bibles

A40

ACTS OF THE APOSTLES

Activity

Teachers will arrange for several study or interest centers for individuals or small groups to:
- —explore key words, questions, or passages;
- —listen to a cassette tape;
- —view a filmstrip;
- —work on a creative activity.

Resource(s)

Bibles, resource books, cassette recorder and tape, filmstrip and projector, creative activity materials **A41**

ACTS OF THE APOSTLES

Activity

Teacher devises a simulation activity that would focus on:
- —the experience of the disciples the day after Pentecost;
- —conflicts between Jews, Gentiles, Romans, Greeks, and Christians;
- —setting standards for who will be accepted into church membership.

Resource(s)

Directions for simulation activity. **A42**

ACTS OF THE APOSTLES

Activity

A cassette recorder could be used by teacher or students to:
- —present directions for an activity;
- —conduct interviews and share them;
- —prepare a script for puppet play or filmstrip;
- —listen to a dramatization, a story, or a Bible passage.

Resource(s)

Cassette recorder and tapes

A43

ACTS OF THE APOSTLES

Activity

Students work on an assignment guided by the following directions:
- —Write a brief job description of what a disciple can expect to do as a follower of Jesus; or
- —Write a brief list of personal characteristics that should be present in a person who would be a disciple.

Resource(s)

Paper and pencils

A44

ACTS OF THE APOSTLES

Activity

A filmstrip could be used by a teacher or students to:
- —present information on a selected topic;
- —select frames for writing a script;
- —focus on a key event, person, or passage;
- —provide a summary.

Resource(s)

Filmstrip, projector, script, and screen

A45

ACTS OF THE APOSTLES

Activity

Students participate in a simulation activity that deals with the question "What do we do now?" Provide a list of five or six possible actions that could be taken in response to a particular event, situation, or issue. Rank items individually, then work in small groups to develop a consensus ranking. Discuss implications for the church today.

Resource(s)

Directions for simulation activity

A46

ACTS OF THE APOSTLES

Activity

Students participate in a creative activity by:
- —producing a set of slides and script;
- —writing articles for a hypothetical newspaper;
- —recording an interview in the style of "You Are There";
- —dramatizing an event.

Resource(s)

Slides, pens, pencils, paper, projector, screen, cassette recorder, tape, etc. **A47**

ACTS OF THE APOSTLES

Activity

Use magazine photographs and headlines to:
- —create a montage;
- —mount as teaching pictures;
- —photograph for slides;
- —develop a story; or
- —use as a contemporary illustration.

Resource(s)

Magazines, paper, scissors, glue, camera, and other necessary resources **A48**

ACTS OF THE APOSTLES

Activity

The teacher provides two lists of passages from Acts—one list related to Peter, the other related to Paul. Several questions are used to analyze and compare the two lists. A discussion follows in order to work at interpreting the passages.

Resource(s)

Lists of passages from Acts and several questions

A49

ACTS OF THE APOSTLES

Activity

An overhead projector can be used:
- —to present information;
- —to do map study;
- —to record responses from students;
- —to provide directions for an activity;
- —to illustrate student reports.

Resource(s)

Overhead projector, screen, transparencies, pens, and pencils

A50

ACTS OF THE APOSTLES

Activity

Teacher and/or students interview pastor or church leaders who come to class as guests. The questions of the interview focus on the tasks of ministry of the particular church. Students are guided to consider ways they can participate actively in the church's ministry.

Resource(s)

Cassette recorder, tape, pencils, paper (optional)

A51

ACTS OF THE APOSTLES

Activity

The teacher presents information or guides students to explore resources related to their church's (denominational and local) convictions regarding the ministry of God's people. Resources such as creeds, confessions, constitutions, catechisms, statements of belief, and hymns are used to focus on responsibilities for ministry and to compare with biblical statements on ministry.

Resource(s)

Printed resources from church documents, Bibles

A52

ACTS OF THE APOSTLES

Activity

Students work together in small groups or as a whole class to decide on one or more specific project(s) or activities they can do in order to participate actively in ministry in the church and/or community.

Resource(s)

None

A53

ACTS OF THE APOSTLES

Activity

Teacher will guide the students to reflect on their own personal understanding of:
- —call to ministry;
- —gifts for ministry, especially their own gifts;
- —responsibilities for ministry;
- —needs of persons requiring responses of caring, helping, and nurturing.

Resource(s)

None

A54

ACTS OF THE APOSTLES

Activity

To summarize or bring closure to a session, the teacher and students can:
- —sing a hymn;
- —participate in a litany prayer;
- —recite a statement of belief;
- —affirm personal convictions;
- —share creative expressions produced earlier.

Resource(s)

None

A55

ACTS OF THE APOSTLES

Activity

(Develop your own activities for any part of the lesson plan.)

Resource(s)

Whatever is needed to implement activities.

A56